PRAYER FOR SPIRITUAL STRENGTH

Physical Illnesses, Emotional Broken Places, and/or Spiritual Dis-eases

The Spiritual Strengths Healing Plan

Richard P. Johnson, Ph.D.

ISBN 978-0-9895130-1-2

10 9 8 7 6 5 4 3 2 1

First Edition

Cover design by Megan Irwin

Edited by Maggie Singleton

Printed in the United States of America

Books in the Spiritual Strengths Healing Series

by Richard P. Johnson

- God Give Me Strength! Finding the Inner Power to Turn Your Illness/Brokenness/Life Transition Around

- Discover Your Spiritual Strengths: Find Health, Healing, and Happiness (flagship book of the Spiritual Strengths Healing Plan)

- Body, Mind, Spirit: Tapping the Healing Power Within

- Prayers for Spiritual Strength: Physical Illnesses, Emotional Broken Places, and/or Spiritual Dis-eases

- The Ten Most Effective Self-Care Healing Techniques: What You Can Do to Maximize Your Healing Journey

- The Power of Smiling: Using Positive Psychology for Optimal Health & Healing

- Healing Wisdom: 101 Spiritual Truths for Healing Your Illness

- Healing and Depression: Finding Peace in the Midst of Transition, Turmoil, or Illness

- Staying Spiritually Centered for Optimal Healing: Even When You're Sick or Life Seems Out of Control

- Seeking Significance: How to Discover New Self-Direction and New Life-Purpose Beyond Your (Unwanted) Life Transition

Caregiving Titles

- Caregiving from Your Spiritual Strengths: The Ten Fundamental Principles for Optimal Success

- Because I Care...Inspiration for Caregiving for Spouses, Health Care Personnel, Family & Friends

The Spiritual Strengths Healing Plan

The Spiritual Strengths Healing Plan allows you to harness your internal healing power! It is not "faith healing" in which one relies on divine intervention as the sole means for physical cure, nor does it promise cure. Its purpose is healing and is best seen as a supplement to and support for current medical practices. The Spiritual Strengths Healing Plan's philosophy holds that each individual needs to seek the best and most appropriate medical and psychological care they can, in accord with their own personal wishes, and supplement their care with this Plan.

Please note that you will see the word "illness" throughout this book in its broadest sense and may indicate any (or a combination) of the following:

I. Physical Sicknesses

Cancer, heart disease, MS, Lupus, migraine, addictions, hypochondriasis, pain, weight management/loss, smoking cessation, pneumonia, COPD, hypertension, arthritis, immune disorders, Parkinson's, diabetes, stroke, chronic fatigue etc., etc.

II. Psychological Issues

Anxiety, depression, personality disorders, OCD, manipulation, stress, bi-polar disorder, etc., etc.

III. Emotional Issues

Being unrealistic, lacking responsibility, low-self-esteem, career focus issues, poor organization skills, family disharmony, anger management, fears, perfectionism, marriage discontent, lifelessness, infidelity, irritability, chronic lateness, caregiving, etc., etc.

IV. Spiritual Dis-eases

Peace of mind and heart, un-forgiveness, existential angst, inner pain, grudges, scrupulosity, incomplete developmental transitions, guilt, grief and unresolved grief, regrets, blame, disappointments, so-called "unfinished business," resentments, etc., etc.

V. Spiritual Direction & Growth

Gaining better clarity of God's plan in your life, and breaking through barriers that may be hindering your faith journey.

Where do <u>you</u> need healing?

For more information about the Spiritual Strengths Healing Plan, log on to...

<u>www.SpiritualStrengthsHealing.com</u>

The Spiritual Strengths Healing Institute

Learning the art of healing for self and others

Contents

Introduction

I wrote the prayers in this book so you could open yourself more fully to God's healing power. Prayer opens us; it widens the portals of our soul so we can better receive the abundance of God's energy/grace; prayer "positions" us so we can better collect God's graces. Prayer makes us more receptive; it softens our soul, prepares our mind, and sensitizes our heart in ways that allow us a fuller flow of grace through God's lifelines of love.

The prayers in this volume are presented in sets of three. The first prayer, or morning prayer, focuses on a particular spiritual strength (virtue). The second prayer, or afternoon prayer, focuses on the "shadow" of that spiritual strength; while the third prayer, the evening prayer, focuses on the "compulsion" of that spiritual strength. While the spiritual strength represents God's direct healing power; the shadow is the opposite of the strength—representing the "absence" of that strength. Finally, the compulsion is a "perversion" of the strength.

Both shadows and compulsions block the power of your spiritual strengths and consequently inhibit your healing. The goal of the Spiritual Strengths Healing Plan is to activate the power of your spiritual strengths and to diminish the effects of the shadows and the compulsions. (Note: For a more thorough description of the spiritual strengths, the shadows, and the compulsions, see chapter two of Discover Your Spiritual Strengths, the "flagship" book of the Spiritual Strengths Healing Plan.)

God heals. God's healing power is omnipotent, all-powerful; omnipresent, everywhere; and omniscient, all knowing. Scripture is full of examples of Christ's healing power. For thousands of years God's healing power has been documented and revered, sought after, praised, elevated, and prayed for. The presence of

God's healing power is undeniable; how to embrace and use this power has always captivated the world's attention.

Research I conducted more than several years ago, when I was the Director of Behavioral Sciences at a large teaching hospital, has instructed me well about the movement and effect of God's healing power in our lives. What I eventually found has not only changed my perception of sickness and healing, but has indeed transformed (healed) my own life as well.

Through this personally moving period in my life, I felt the hand of God on mine, urging me to write what I had seen in these marvelous spiritually-healing patients. I became the scribe; I honestly feel that God moved my hands, not in any automatic writing phenomenon, but clearly I was guided to organize what I had observed into a coherent and practical program. Over the years, I have given innumerable healing workshops and talks, all of which helped me refine this organization of ideas and revelations, until it has taken the form it has today, in what I call The Spiritual Strengths Healing Plan.

This prayer book is part of a series of books that all serve to describe and extend the Spiritual Strengths Healing Plan toward one end: to make the program as accessible and as useful to God's children who are dealing with the effects of any sickness, affliction, condition, brokenness, emotional tumult, psychological distress, and/or spiritual dis-ease to find healing. I offer you this program in the hopes that it will bring you new life and new spirit.

Blessings to you,

R. P. Johnson

How to Best Use This Book

You can use this prayer book in several ways...

1. Use it as a one-month self-directed mini-retreat reciting and meditating on each of the 30 sets of three prayers, one set per day for a month.

2. Use it as a prayer reference by opening to any page for prayerful inspiration and/or psychological motivation.

3. The most comprehensive, targeted and effective way to use this book is as an integral part of what I call the...

Spiritual Strengths Healing Plan

Step 1: Take the SSHP

Take the Spiritual Strengths Healing Profile (SSHP) available at www.spiritualstrengthshealing.com. The SSHP takes about 20-25 minutes to complete and it generates a 20-page personal analysis of your spiritual strengths that gives you a new depth of self-understanding so you quite naturally begin moving toward healing. You'll discover your six "premier spiritual strengths" as well as the shadows and compulsions that accompany them. These six strengths are the virtues that God has given to you most clearly at this stage in your life so you can make the most of whatever that life is bringing you at this time. These six constitute your personal formula for achieving maximal healing.

Step 2: "Discover Your Spiritual Strengths" Book

Procure the reference book Discover Your Spiritual Strengths: Find Health, Healing & Happiness. This is the "flagship" book of the Spiritual Strengths Healing Plan series of books; you will want this book for reference as you move through the Plan. If you want to go deeper, then proceed to...

Step 3: The Spiritual Strengths Healing Immersion Program

Procure your own Spiritual Strengths Healing Immersion Program at www.spiritualstrengthshealing.com. This is an individualized, seven-week program made especially for you based on your specific and unique six spiritual strengths. The Immersion Program asks you to spend about 15 minutes per day for seven weeks. The Program allows God's healing power to penetrate deeply into you. You become saturated as you soak in the warm, cleansing, and healing waters of your spiritual strengths. Your daily time with your spiritual strengths nourishes your heart, mind, and soul in ways that bring you to a brand new level of healing.

Step 4: Prayer

The prayers in this book can be used anytime, anywhere, and in any way you find them helpful. Perhaps the best way to use these prayers is to use them in conjunction with Step #3 (above) by devoting each day of the week to a different one of your premier healing strengths. You are asked to pray your spiritual strength prayer in the morning, its corresponding shadow prayer in the afternoon, and its compulsion prayer in the evening. This organized approach, used in conjunction with the SSHP and the other reading material that is part of the Plan, offers you the consistency and regularity that is essential for inviting healing grace into your life during this expansive time.

Step 5: Follow Through

Work through the seven-week program. I know from my clinical experience with hundreds of persons seeking healing that following the 7-Week Immersion Program does bring results...I can almost guarantee it if you remain faithful to the Program.

Trust the process of the program...
it will change you if you let it!

Sickness vs. Illness

So often we confuse these two words: sickness and illness. We use them interchangeably as though they each meant the same thing. They don't!

Sickness is when a part of the body is broken or malfunctioning. Any medical diagnosis or psychiatric malady is a sickness. Diabetes, for example, is a sickness!

Illness, on the other hand, refers to any of your personal, emotional, psychological, and/or spiritual reactions to your sickness. Any and all of your negative emotional, psychological, relational, and other reactions to your sickness is your illness.

The Spiritual Strengths Healing Plan is NOT designed to
cure your sickness; rather it is designed to heal the illness
of your sickness. These are two very different goals.

The medical community is charged with curing your sickness, whatever it is; and it is working overtime in its attempts to cure sickness in general. Some sicknesses are curable, others are not. As of this writing the search for the cure for many sicknesses has proven elusive despite all the resources, both financial and technological, that our culture has so far expended on this noble endeavor. Someday all sickness may be cured, until then we do the best we can. Healing the illness caused by our sickness is the first priority of this program.

Short periods of prayer three times a day are essential for
the success of your seven-week healing program.

Prayer: Our Primary Healing Mechanism

Our primary curing mechanism is medicine, while our primary healing mechanism is prayer. We can seek and use both curing and healing with deliberate care, with informed focus, and with considered choice. When we use it liberally and intelligently, medicine, in all its forms, serves us well. Likewise, we are called to prayer; we're especially called in times of trial when we need to be as open as possible to the healing power of God's grace. Although not its primary purpose, prayer may add to the efficacy of medical treatment in many ways.

- Prayer has the power to transform us—making us more resilient to the barrage of discomfort that sickness brings.

- Prayer is a mighty force for promoting our own health and well-being.

- Prayer, due to its introspective nature, is a sound psychological process as well as a spiritually uplifting one.

- Prayer allows us to come to a fuller realization of our own God-given powers and to focus them more clearly on our current situation.

Dr. Randolph Byrd conducted perhaps the most startling study on prayer and healing (which can be seen at http://www.iwriteiam.nl/D960916-prayer.html). He studied heart patients by first dividing them into two groups for research purposes. One group was prayed for by a group of ministers and lay persons; the other group enjoyed no such intercessory prayer. At the termination of the completely blind study (neither the patients knew they were being prayed for, nor did the "pray-ers" know who they were praying for...all were "blind"), Dr. Byrd found that those who received prayer suffered significantly fewer complications; they required much less medication to control side effects; they were much less likely to suffer congestive heart failure; and they had a significantly lower risk of sudden cardiac arrest. Other studies have substantiated that the connection between prayer and health seems real.

Healing requires something that may seem obvious, but unfortunately many times it isn't obvious at all—you must recognize that you need healing. Healing is certainly as important, if not more important, than curing. The degree to which you don't see the need for healing is the same degree to which you block healing.

It's easy to recognize when you're sick... you don't feel well! In addition to the physical symptoms you experience, the medical community has codified so many of these symptoms into actual medical diagnoses. Consequently, you are diagnosed with diabetes or heart disease, diverticulitis or shingles, arthritis or peptic ulcers, cancer, and so forth.

On the other hand, it's not so easy to determine when you're ill, when your response to your sickness requires healing. You may think it quite unusual to realize that physical symptoms are attended by emotional symptoms. For example, you may not find it surprising that persons with chronic sickness become depressed or anxious or contentious or denying or irritable, or any of a number of reactions that you can understand. But do you think of these reactions as indicators of an illness that requires healing? Probably not!

Dr. Larry Dossey, M.D. has written an intriguing book entitled Healing Words, (Harper San Francisco, 1993). Dr. Dossey says that prayer can guide and sustain us so we can courageously confront our trials. He maintains that prayer is our primary tool for addressing the fear and anxiety that generally accompanies sickness, especially protracted sickness.

Prayer can so vitalize us that the severity of our ailments seems to lessen considerably. Perhaps the most widely used form of prayer is intercessory prayer, where we seek a specific outcome. When we ask God for a cure to our affliction, a remedy for our maladies, or a cessation to our sickness, we are engaging in intercessory prayer. Dr. Dossey points out that intercessory prayer can be rather presumptuous on our part; in effect, we are telling God what to do.

Dr. Dossey contrasts this with what he calls prayerfulness. "Prayerfulness is accepting without being passive, is grateful without giving up. It is more willing to stand in the mystery, to tolerate ambiguity and the unknown. It honors the rightness of whatever happens, even sickness." (page 24). This form of prayer, or this state of being in prayer, is what Dr. Dossey seems to favor in his work. *"Prayerfulness allows us to reach a plane of experience where illness (and sickness) can be experienced as a natural part of life, and where its acceptance transcends passivity. If the disease disappears, we are grateful; if it remains, that too is reason for gratitude."* (page 27).

Dr. Dossey tackles a persistently knotty question that always emerges when healing prayer is discussed: Is there a special formula, some universal form, type, or sequence of prayer that will "work" for all persons? Dossey's response, after reviewing hundreds of medical research projects, is clearly in the negative. He advocates prayer that renews our personal commitment to God and is plentifully laced with gratitude for God's love, combined with a deep acceptance, but not submission or resignation, of God's will being done, regardless of the outcome.

Dr. Dossey claims that persons who seem most successful in achieving healing through prayer do not follow some regulated formula or strict sequence; they do not engage in a mindless, heartless, and soulless rote method of prayer. Rather they pray intentionally from their whole being, from their heart and soul, from the spiritual uniqueness that is their own. Dossey writes: *"Get-well formulas that advocate spiritual practices are by definition inauthentic because they require that one take on spirituality from the outside, instead of allowing it to emerge from the center of one's being."* (page 32).

Dr. Dossey's thesis seems to be that the real gift of healing prayer is arriving at a fuller appreciation of one's "higher self," the presence of God within us, and a heightened communion with God as a consequence of our sickness. Ultimately, we come to realize that the true reality of ourselves is not simply physical but also spiritual; and that our true, genuine self is impervious to disease because it lives forever. I've intended this book as your personal springboard from which you can continue your own unique prayer journey.

Another View of Faith

We see a different view of the power of prayer through the eyes of Dr. Harold G. Koenig, M.D. in his book The Healing Power of Faith. (Simon & Schuster, New York, 1999). Dr. Koenig approaches prayer from a decidedly more scientific perspective. As the Director of the Duke University Center for the Study of Religion/Spirituality and Health, Dr. Koenig uses scientific research methods demanding highly rigorous investigative methods. Dr. Koenig is particularly interested in the role of prayer, church attendance, and other faith practices in bolstering our physical health and well being.

Dr. Koenig was impressed with the research done by Dr. Herbert Benson of Harvard who studied the effects of religiously-oriented prayer as compared to nonreligious meditation. Dr. Benson found that each has similar positive relaxation effects, but that most people favor prayer over meditation because they find it to be more emotionally comforting than nonreligious meditation.

Dr. Koenig set out to investigate what other value prayer might offer for the health and well-being of maturing adults. He found plenty! Dr. Koenig found that religious activity and prayer contributed mightily to overall happiness (what we call life satisfaction) and good morale. These two factors do much more than simply provide emotional comfort; they are positively correlated to our physical health in general, and contribute to *"an optimistic sense of purpose within God's plan."* (page 41). This finding has far reaching implications for health. His research findings indicate that *"...a strong personal faith directly shields people from life's inevitable problems, which in turn increase a sense of well-being."* (page 42).

Dr. Koenig goes on to present startling research data from a variety of settings that comprehensively and scientifically describe the positive impacts that religious faith and prayer have on many, many different physical and emotional maladies. The research presented by Dr. Koenig points to the value of prayer as an important factor in the success of marriage. In the area of coping and stress reduction, Dr. Koenig sites research which found that persons of strong faith cope better under even the direst circumstances, they are buoyed by their relationship with God and feel the comfort of the bonds with their faith community. He points out that faith can transform the discouragement and hopelessness of any life trial, including sickness, into hope and strength.

Depression is the number one emotional illness of those suffering from sickness. Depression can emerge in a person's life as a consequence of the illness of helplessness that sometimes overtakes a person as a result of sickness. Some of us are genetically predisposed to depression and are therefore more prone to it. Dr. Koenig's research indicates that even though prayerful people suffer from depression at the same incidence rate as others, the severity of the depression and its duration are significantly less among people who pray. (page 132). Dr. Koenig states, *"I believe, however, that religious faith can become a cost-*

effective complement to psychotherapy and medication in this effort." (page 148).

Dr. Koenig continues in his book citing numerous correlations between religious attendance, prayer and various facets of health that hard-data scientific research has high-lighted the following surprising findings:

1. Religiously active people live longer and healthier lives.

2. People who regularly pray are 40% less likely to have high blood pressure than those who don't.

3. Adults who are both socially active and who find strength and comfort in their faith are 14 times <u>less</u> likely to die up to six months after major surgery.

4. Adults who attend religious services have stronger immune systems that those who do not.

5. People who attend church at least once per week are 43% less likely to have been admitted to the hospital in the prior year than the less religious participants.

6. Frequent religious service attenders spend fewer days in the hospital; those with no religious affiliation spent an average of 14 more days in the hospital.

His compilation of hard-data research presents persuasive evidence that practicing our faith, through church attendance and prayer has bona fide positive effects on our health and well-being in many facets of life.

Research like Dr. Koenig's gives our modern intellectually-critical mindset dramatic proof of what we only could intuitively infer previously – that we can indeed influence our overall well-being through prayer. While the possibility of imposing upon God to perform a miracle by curing our sickness may be remote, there seems little doubt that prayer, especially intrinsic prayer from our heart, can and does aid us in healing our illnesses.

Again, the mechanisms of curing are drugs, surgery, and rehabilitation procedures, while the primary mechanism of healing is prayer in all its various forms.

- Prayer brings us into more intimate and conscious contact with God, and opens us to God's healing power of grace.

- Prayer positions us to receive the maximum benefit from the abundant treasure of healing grace that God provides for us every day.

- Prayer mends our spiritual afflictions and our moral infirmities. Prayer re-energizes a heart grown limp, a mind grown dim and lazy, and a spirit grown uninspired.

- Prayer motivates us on the psychological and spiritual levels to bring our best giftedness forward into the light.

But in order for healing to begin, we must be very aware that healing is required. We need to acknowledge that we are suffering in mind and spirit; otherwise the plentiful healing grace of God cannot enter into us.

Certainly most of us want to avoid the discomfort and pain that comes with sickness; we either want to prevent sickness from invading us, or if sickness does descend upon us, we want to push it out of our lives as soon as possible. Yet we can't always do that.

Some sickness is chronic, it has no particular end. Indeed, much sickness has some degree of chronicity; even flu can hang on for a long time; there are some strains of flu that can make us more susceptible to contracting it again. Other sickness is more clearly chronic, we can never cure it; in medical terms, we simply "manage" it. Consider the chronic nature of: diabetes, arthritis, MS, lupus, stroke, most heart disease, liver or kidney damage,

COPD (chronic obstructive pulmonary disease), Parkinson's disease, many types of cancer, immunodeficiency disorders, some depressions, cerebellar ataxia, and the dreaded Alzheimer's disease. Modern medical science has found no cure for these, and many, many other sicknesses; all we can do is treat the symptoms and alleviate as much of the pain that comes with it as we can.

Praying for a cure of a sickness is asking for a miracle, asking God to change the course of nature. Certainly God has the power to do this, and many ask why God doesn't lift the sickness from them, saying 'if God is a benevolent God, He would undoubtedly lift this terrible burden from my life.' Yet, people suffer from chronic diseases every day. Is this testimony that God is not benevolent, kind, merciful, generous, and steadfast? Certainly not! We live in mystery; our logic is not God's.

How curious was Jesus' answer to his disciples regarding the man born blind. Jesus said that the blind man's affliction was not the result of his parent or his grandparent's sin, but that he was so afflicted for the greater glory of God (John 9). Jesus more than implied that there is a higher purpose for sickness, even chronic sickness; a purpose which we are called to accept, if not understand, as we mature in our faith.

What is this higher value or purpose of sickness? Perhaps sickness is not simply a cruelty; perhaps it has a message, a lesson for us that stands just beyond the actual sickness. We are called to delve deeply into our soul so we can investigate with all due diligence what this purpose might be for our lives. Yet, our sometimes faulty human logic may cause us to jump to the conclusion that because there may be a lesson in our sickness that the Holy Spirit chose to give us the sickness, with all its attendant pain and suffering, just so we could learn this lesson. This would indeed seem cruel to most of us.

God loves us no less whether we are physically healthy or not. Perhaps the Holy Spirit is using the random and quite natural occurrence of our sickness and brokenness as an opportunity for our learning, a means of growing closer to God and more comfortable with ourselves; not the other way around!

Certainly we'd rather not have our sicknesses, but praying for a cure may be in some way thwarting the very real possibility that the Holy Spirit is using our sickness to bring us closer to God. In this light, praying for a cure may be presumptuous on our part in that it represents our attempt at telling God what we think is best for us rather than listening to what God may be trying to teach us.

We are called to listen deeply inside of ourselves on the occasion of our sickness. Indeed, if sickness can be seen as a form of poverty, a kind of poverty of health; as strange as it may at first seem, could our sickness actually be a form of blessing since we know that Jesus seemed to favor the poor at every turn in his earthly life; and when we are sick, we are poor!

The Characteristics of Healing Prayer

Does "praying for a cure" differ substantially from "praying for healing?" Praying for a cure refers to our attempt to petition God; asking God to lift our sickness from us completely. By contrast, "praying for healing" involves seeking healing grace: the strength, the stamina, the hope, the faith, etc. necessary for us to meet the challenges presented to us by our sickness. We take a very different spiritual posture and make very different assumptions about the purpose of our prayer when we engage in one or the other.

1. With curing prayer we request a very specific outcome, an outcome that we define ourselves. The goal of curing prayer is for our sickness to "go away," to be removed from our lives. In contrast, healing prayer places the outcome of

our sickness in God's hands. We are requesting in our prayer that we "get out of the Holy Spirit's way", as it were, and let God's Will take the lead in our lives.

2. Curing prayer is rather directive and somewhat controlling. It represents our attempt at imposing our own will onto God's. In contrast, healing prayer is accepting God's Will. This type of acceptance is not submission, nor is it resignation, each of these is a form of abdication of our own free will; something God does not want for us.

3. Curing prayer does attribute power to God, but it paradoxically assumes that we retain the directive executive power of running our lives ourselves. Curing prayer is essentially self-centered. Curing prayer starts from the self and focuses only on the self. Contrast this to healing prayer that is God-centered, it clearly recognizes God's ultimate omnipotence. It gives all power to God.

4. Curing prayer is seen as a specific task; we spend a certain limited amount of time in petition prayer, and see our "work" as done; we have done our job as it were. By contrast, healing prayer involves a more or less sustained attitude of prayerfulness that we carry with us wherever we go. We live in a continuous prayer.

5. Curing prayer seems intolerant of mystery, it seeks to influence reality, to plan, and to rationalize; it attempts to inject logic and reason into an arena that is mysterious at its core. Healing prayer, on the other hand, recognizes that we walk in mystery; we recognize that our life is indefinable and unpredictable.

6. Curing prayer is seen primarily as a spiritual "drug" that we take to alleviate the physical symptoms of sickness. Healing prayer is seen as primarily building communion with God, as

becoming ever more intimate with God as the basis of our life, and the primary course we need to follow.

7. Curing prayer is extrinsic, external, and somewhat detached. Curing prayer emanates from the head; it sees the source of healing as a function of the world with little or no personal involvement. Healing prayer is intrinsic, internal and personal. Healing prayer emanates from the heart and soul; it sees the source of healing as the power of God manifested internally.

8. Curing prayer can be impatient and tends to see sickness as a disaster, an intruder, and a tragedy. Healing prayer is patient and sees sickness as a master teacher.

9. Curing prayer sees the purpose of prayer as the end of sickness. Healing prayer, by contrast, sees the purpose of prayer as becoming more who we really are.

10. Curing prayer sees human life, continued existence on this plane as the highest good. Healing prayer sees eternal life, salvation, as the highest good.

The Diamond of Love

Where curing seeks to "fix" the body, healing brings a soothing and relief-filled balm not primarily to the body but to the mind, heart, and spirit. Healing calls forth the power that only comes from God; power like: hope and charity, acceptance and kindness, mercy and perseverance, simplicity and empathy. Such powers are different facets of the diamond of love that focus laser-like healing to the root of the problem and bring transformative energy to the site of the suffering.

PRAYERS

FOR

Spiritual Strength

Section One

The Believing Function

The Believing Function

These five spiritual strengths are the love-energy, or grace, that allows you to believe clearly, accurately, "rightly," and thereby position you to best bring healing (through God's grace) to your illness. One of these is your premier spiritual strength (as identified by your personal SSHP), which means that, for whatever reason, this spiritual strength is the most prominent, the most powerful for you at this time. You do have the other four in your personality, but at this time in your life they are of somewhat lessened power than your premier spiritual strength. Under each spiritual strength you will find its shadow, (the absence of the strength), and its compulsion (or perversion of the strength).

NOTE: Personalize this book by inserting your own illness, sickness, disease, disorder, or personal brokenness in the underlined space in each prayer throughout this book.

Morning Prayer
God-Reliance

You are the beginning and the end of my life, the Alpha and the Omega.

God, you are the fountain of all goodness, all virtue, and all energy.

Today I seek to capture the fullness of your gift of God-Reliance as my ultimate means for finding my way in this world, and certainly through my current travail of _____.

You are the beginning and end of my life, the Alpha and Omega. You are the rock upon which I can rely in all disturbing times.

I want dearly to believe entirely and thoroughly in you, to see with your eyes, think with your mind, feel with your heart, choose with your will, and act with your hands.

I center the entire value system of my belief core on you and around you. Now, more than ever, I need your strength to find union with you.

By your omnipotent energy of love, I find the power and might to always be in solidarity with you. I do not simply *believe* in you, Lord. I *know* in you. I am utterly convicted of your active role in my life.

I seek your help in sustaining my complete reliance on you as the indomitable foundation of my being, the cornerstone which you have planted in me from time immemorial.

Amen

Afternoon Prayer

Doubt

The Shadow of God-Reliance

Help me overcome my doubt, my skepticism, and my uncertainty.

Lord, I seek release from the turmoil and torture of any remnants of the shadow of doubt.

With your grace, help me lighten the burden of my questioning mind that leads me to dispute what I know is right.

You are the first source and center of the cosmos; you are the creator of all and the primal force that sustains everything.

You are the only source of love, and love is the only reality in the universe.

Help me overcome my distrust, skepticism, and uncertainty.

Sustain me through my unbelief, and carry me beyond my need to control the uncontrollable.

Be with me Lord when I falter in my belief and I agitate my

_____.

Be my rock of security when I stray and lose sight of my core conviction that you are everything.

Save me from my tendencies to rush to judgment, a place within me where I only suffer from self-imposed isolation.

Amen

Evening Prayer

Dependency

The Compulsion of God-Reliance

I have many dependencies, yet all of them are unreal, except my need for you, Lord.

Lord, I pray that you offer me the power of God-Reliance to reduce my excessive needs.

I need only you, because you are the foundation of my soul, the rock of my security.

All my supposed needs are but artificial facsimiles of my one and only need ...You!

I'm so tempted to see my value only in terms of those around me, or in my achievements.

I have developed many dependencies, and all of them are unreal, except my need for you, Lord.

When I subordinate my spirit only to the desires of others, I block your healing power from my _____.

Help me gain confidence in you, Lord, so I can stop giving my decisions away to the sways and swings of the world.

I know that you are the only rock, you are the only surety, and you are the only certainty that exists, Lord.

Help me "be" in you, and believe completely in you, always.

Amen

Morning Prayer
Humility

Today I am free from confusion about who I am, because I now know who I am.

Good morning, Lord. I dedicate myself to do and be your will.

Today I seek to be nothing other than what I authentically am.

Humility calls me to be real, to claim my hurts but also to claim my strengths equally.

Help me not forget that I am gifted, and that your gifts in me yearn to be exercised, lest I lose them.

Humility calls me to be true to myself, my True Self, not the facsimile ego self that sometimes masquerades around as me.

I am first and foremost your child, Lord; all else is meager and transitory, only time-limited roles I play here on this plane.

Only you define my real self, Lord. Humility calls me to honor that real self as the only true definition of me.

I am in this world to discover the truest reality of me, the love you have invested in me.

Today, in the name of humility, I will take off any masks that I've been wearing, and take down any facades that I may have constructed that may block healing from my _____.

In this way I am free from worry and confusion about who I am, because I now know who I am.

Amen

Afternoon Prayer

Self-Centeredness

The Shadow of Humility

Lord, allow me to "own" my own truth, which is your truth within me.

Save me, Lord, from my ferocious need to puff myself up, to be different from the truth of who I am.

Spare me, through your gift of humility, so I can turn away from my desires to be other than what and who I am.

Let your humility pull me toward your authenticity and my own, and heal my _____.

Help me avoid my vulnerability to model myself after what the world sees as beautiful, or sexy, or strong, or powerful, or trendy, or any other such illusions.

Help me model myself after you alone.

Lord, allow me to "own" my own truth, which is actually your truth within me, and not indulge in self-love above loving you.

I know that your strength can foil my conceit, eradicate my complacency, and defuse my exaggerated self-importance.

Help me see beyond my tendency toward selfishness.

Amen

Evening Prayer

Self-Abasement

The Compulsion of Humility

Self-abasement closes me off from my own true reality.

Lord, grant me a stronger grip on your strength of humility in me so I can get out from under the burdensome weight of fearing the scrutiny of others.

I know for sure that humility does release me from my compulsion of self-abasement; true humility rolls away the heavy stones of inferiority, shame, and guilt that I've been carrying far too long.

Humility offers me blessed healing of my _____.

Self-abasement closes me off from my own true reality.

Your humility in me allows me to know the rightness of my own convictions and frees me from always believing that the thoughts of others are better than my own.

I so want and need your grace to emancipate me from my lack of faith in the strengths that you have already given me; help me capture your grace, Lord.

I no longer wish to neglect myself by overlooking your promise of love. I know that I can begin to believe in the true me like I never have before.

Amen

Morning Prayer
Acceptance

Today I offer you my complete "Amen"

Oh, what a happy day it is, knowing that you are with me, Lord.

Today my only goal is to live in your love, to be in your holy strength of acceptance.

I aspire to be nothing less than your sacred acceptance today.

Lord, I long to live in perfect accord with only you.

I seek only to align my truth with yours.

Today I offer you my complete "amen."

I utter the words of holy acceptance, not as resignation or submission but as the true spiritual "grit" that affirms me as the "me" that you desire.

Today I know your authority over me is a holy act of kindness that fully knows what and who I am, and only desires that I live in your abundance.

Help me to fully accept your plan for my life and aspire to live it out as best I can today.

I offer you my _____ to do with it as you wish, knowing that your wishes are always in my best interest; help me carry-out this conviction the whole day through.

Amen

Afternoon Prayer

Dissension

The Shadow of Acceptance

I seek only to flow with your holy currents of grace and not against them.

Lord, lift the terrible weight of dissension from me.

I wander away from you every time I disagree with your gentle direction, every time I turn away in unexamined resistance.

I want to accept your will, Lord, and not continuously fight what I know without question is good for me.

Help me shake my adolescent need to be at-odds with others and with your desires for me.

I seek only to flow with, not against, your holy currents of grace as my shadow of dissension lures me to do.

My dissension keeps my _____ in the director's seat of my personality.

Keep me from hostility of any kind, against others or against myself; and most of all, keep me from being hostile to you, Lord.

Help me to stay in line with you and not at variance from you.

Help me stop fighting all those paper dragons of my own making, Lord.

Amen

Evening Prayer

Aloofness

The Compulsion of Acceptance

Help me to connect rather than detach from others, myself, and You.

Stir me up, Lord, so that I can rest in the warm love of you, and not distance myself from you in some chilly and dispassionate avoidance.

Being cool makes my life a bit colder, as well as aloof from others around me.

Help me to connect rather than detach from others, and from myself.

Sometimes I'm afraid of sustained and close interaction, and so I unknowingly protect myself from imagined harm by giving others a cold shoulder of aloofness.

Break me of my habit to remove myself, and keep me united with others instead of feeling the defensive need to "fly solo."

But Lord, my most terrible aloofness is when I distance myself from you, when I absurdly believe that I can "go it alone" without you, or even confuse myself into believing that my will is somehow better than yours!

My compulsion to separate myself also separates me from your power to heal my _____.

Amen

Morning Prayer
Mercy

Help me extend my hand as your hand to others today, Lord.

As the sun breaks through and warms the earth this morning, by your grace I reassert my conviction that mercy is the essential power in my life today, Lord.

I seek compassion, forbearance, and tenderness toward others and myself in your grace of mercy.

Help me extend my hand to others as your hand —offering them the fullness of your power and presence.

Today I seek recognize and practice mercy everywhere: from humanitarian giving to empathic listening, and from leniency to true pity.

Motivate me to see the plight of others and act to soothe their pain only in your Spirit.

Help me fill my being and saturate my entire personality with your mercy.

Lord, help me be humane and just today, just as your power of mercy is tender and caring as it massages my _____ with healing.

Grant me your strength of forgiving mercy.

Today I long to "be" your mercy, both to myself and to others.

Amen

Afternoon Prayer

Indifference

The Shadow of Mercy

*Release me from the demon of indifference;
only your grace can save me.*

Lord, help me remove the fangs from my shadow of indifference.

Let me be attentive not bored, decisive not lack-luster, active in you not lazy, and vital not careless.

Lord, please cleanse me of my terrible indifference that blocks your hand from touching and healing my _____.

Indifference pushes me away from those in need, and it lures me to a defensive criticism of those who most require help.

Indifference keeps me silent when I could say a kind word; it stops me from caring, and it hardens my heart.

I seek release from this demon, Lord; only your grace can save me.

I need your consoling hand to awaken me from the somnolence of indifference.

Make me uncomfortable with myself when I'm tempted to turn a blind eye, or when I criticize rather than be moved by true pity.

Give me the strength of mercy to overcome my oppressive indifference.

Amen

Evening Prayer

Legalism

The Compulsion of Mercy

I can, at times, be stubborn and stiff-necked, demanding, and excessively strict.

Lord, I seek your grace to extract me from the pit of over-reliance on standards and rules, regulations, and laws as the primary authority of my life.

I know that you are the only authority, but too often, out of fear, I seek the authority of human experts and/or cultural standards as my guiding principles for living, rather than you.

I falter when I fall victim to our worldly media that overlooks the authenticity of your teaching.

Save me from the confusion of legalism, Lord.

I sometimes hold myself and others to overly strict "rules" of thinking and behavior; I demand that others conform to my beliefs; I negate their thinking by not truly listening to them.

I can, at times, be stubborn and stiff-necked, demanding, and excessively strict. Save me in these times of trial.

Save me from imposing this loathsome legalism on everything: others, institutions, the Church, people in authority, on myself, and also on you, Lord.

Legalism undermines your healing touch on my _____.

Amen

Morning Prayer
Hope

The splendor of the virtue of hope lights my way and leads me to you today.

God, I know that you are the architect of my soul.

You chose to place the power of hope in me, and I know that you expect me to be a whole fragment of your hope for the world.

I know that I am most happy, healthy, and holy when I'm in love with you in hope.

Let me greet this day with the enthusiasm and optimism that flows only from your hope.

Help me always respond in your hope and not react with my shadow of despair or my compulsive presumption.

The splendor of the virtue of hope lights my way and leads me to you today. In that journey I know I will find healing of my _____ in hope; I will find it in me and around me, all reflections of you, Lord.

Propelled by your gift of hope I have absolute assurance that your power of love can never be eclipsed; there is no power in the universe stronger than your love.

I have a deep conviction that your love will always remain the compelling power in the cosmos.

Amen

Afternoon Prayer

Despair

The Shadow of Hope

*I always need your hope to regain my bearings
and find the center of my soul.*

The realization that I have strayed from your gift of hope startles and shakes me, Lord.

I can find myself slipping toward despair in so many ways.

I need, always need, your hope to regain my bearings and find the center of my soul.

Lord, you know that I can become irritable, disillusioned, and even dreary and flat at times.

Grant me your hope, Lord, especially when I slide away from hope and feel sad, melancholy, and weary.

Grant me your hope, Lord; I can sometimes even feel empty, fatigued, and guilty.

Grant me your hope, Lord; spare me from sliding all the way from you, with my back to the wall in abject hopelessness, somehow believing that my _____ has conquered me.

This is not the real me and certainly this is not what you want for me.

Activate my hope, and save me from the abyss of despair.

Amen

Evening Prayer

Presumption

The Compulsion of Hope

Save me from thinking that I can somehow save myself.

Lord, I don't know that I'm moving toward presumption until I actually get there. Help me recognize when I'm slipping; help me access your hope to catch me, at least to become more aware that I'm moving in that direction.

Lord, help me surmount my vulnerability of taking things for granted. Help me temper my tendency to "know it all" or to think that my thoughts and ideas are simply "better."

Help me resist taking liberties that are not mine to take.

I can take undeserved credit for "my" accomplishments when actually you, not me, are the engineer and prime mover.

I seem to have a built-in belief that I'm entitled to favored treatment, which only blocks my growth and healing.

Save me from believing that I can somehow save myself; that somehow my "successes" come from my own work and not from you.

Lord, help me believe in the real me and not the presumed me; and in that conversion, may I find healing of my _____ in you.

Amen

Section Two

The Perceiving Function

The Perceiving Function

Only rarely are you aware of your awareness. Your outlook on the world; and your insight into self is accomplished, for the most part, without the slightest recognition of what you're doing. Perceptions just seem to happen without any intention or volition on your part, yet how you frame or image what you encounter directs your life. What you choose to focus upon, and how you choose to frame it becomes your world; your perceptions make the world in which you live.

Your premier perceiving spiritual strength draws you toward the truth, while the shadow and compulsion of your perceiving premier strength pulls you toward unreality. It's only in reality where you can find healing. Healing calls you to an awareness of that which is beyond the material plane. Healing beckons you to stretch to a farther horizon of awareness, to see the divinity that is the driving force of your personality (page 95, Discover Your Spiritual Strengths: Find Health, Healing & Happiness).

Morning Prayer
Vision

I can catch a glimpse of the eternal, a reflection of heaven, right here.

This morning I awaken from my sleepiness to discover a new world of color and detail, of enhanced hue and brightness, a newness of which I was previously unaware.

Today I can sense your presence keener, Lord, as I see through the powerful lens of the strength of your vision.

I know, from the depth of my core, that you offer me pearls of light that contain the power to heal me of my _____.

I see things with ever-finer clarity as I grow closer to you.

You do indeed make all things new, Lord.

Vision allows me to see a reflection of your face just beyond the material world.

Today I sense your presence anew; and in my mind's eye, I imagine you everywhere.

It's as though I can catch a glimpse of the eternal, a reflection of heaven, right here...right now.

I literally see things differently; I see your hand in everything, everywhere, and in everyone.

Lord, help me stay centered in your vision all day long.

Amen

Afternoon Prayer

Blindedness

The Shadow of Vision

Help me focus on what is of you, Lord, and away from what is not.

Oh …do I wish release from the shadow of blindedness.

Help me Lord, open my eyes and sharpen all my senses so I don't fall into darkness today.

Enhance my limited perception and enrich my imagination so I can see your points of light inside me overtaking any darkness there.

Blindedness makes me insecure and clumsy; it causes me to stumble over the same nothingness that I stumbled over yesterday, and yesterday, and the yesterday before that.

Help me focus on what is of you, Lord, and away from what is not.

Take the logs from my eyes that distort my vision and deaden my soul.

Help me search only for what is real.

Let me see with your eyes, Lord, so that I can once again see clearly.

Through the marvelous mystery of your grace help me find you, and there discover healing for my _____.

Amen

Evening Prayer

Illusion

The Compulsion of Vision

Shift my point of view so I can perceive "rightly."

Why do I make real what is not, Lord?

Why do I focus on things of the world like contention, jealousy, shame, anger, twisted motivation, arrogance, distrust, fear, and the like when I want to focus on the real truth which is only of you?

Help my distorted vision see what is real from what is mere illusion. Shift my point of view so I can perceive "rightly."

I seek the true meaning of things and not some facsimile that is but an illusion of truth. Help me see through your lens of life so I can see clearly, not darkly.

When I can perceive my _____ accurately, I discover that your hand is there working-in the balm of healing grace.

When I see my hurts only as terrorists, I'm in illusion and don't see the teacher that resides there. Help me to see through the illusions of the world and view all of your creation as essentially good and not fearsome.

I know that you wish that I live my life in abundance; seeing accurately is a step toward that abundance.

Amen

Morning Prayer

Humor

I can almost see God smiling at me.

Today I awaken to my authentic self; that place in me where the Spirit resides, and I smile broadly because I recognize how silly I can be sometimes.

I'm moved to laugh at my foibles, quirks, and inconsistencies of thought and behavior.

When I see myself clearly I recognize how laughable some of my behaviors really are.

If I don't find humor in these personal idiosyncrasies, then I only find self-condemnation.

I chuckle at myself when I come to appreciate the view of me as I think God sees me.

God doesn't look at me with an eye for what's wrong; God only sees what's right, and good, and precious.

I can almost make out God smiling at me.

Just as a mother might smile at her child's mistake, or find comical a bit of "cute" behavior.

Lord, continue the flow of your grace of humor so I can see all of me, and especially my _____ in the holy light of a joyful viewpoint.

Let your light of humor push away all in me that is not of you.

Amen

Afternoon Prayer

Lamentation

The Shadow of Humor

*Strengthen me with holy humor, your grace
that opens me beyond lamentation.*

Save me from the different forms of woe that I perpetrate on myself, Lord.

Bless me with your grace—that point of light called humor that you placed within me.

Help me recognize when I'm inching away from humor and over to the shadow of lamentation.

Help turn me around and away from self-pity, away from whining and grumbling, and away from complaint and criticism.

Grant me a new view of my _____ so I don't become trapped in a vortex of helplessness.

Awaken me to your sacred illumination that soothes and even heals me of the terrible woes of hopelessness that threaten to overtake me at times.

Strengthen me with holy humor, your celestial grace that opens me beyond the confines of lamentation.

Help me see the humor in my foibles and experience the full power of your care in me.

Amen

Evening Prayer

Recklessness

The Compulsion of Humor

Let me not poke fun at others, belittle, or mock them with a vicious chuckle or smirk.

Oh Lord, help me surmount my vulnerability toward recklessness, that terrible compulsion that perverts your beautiful gift of humor into an underhanded means of gaining false stature.

I can use recklessness to cut others down by making fun of them.

I can sometimes cover over my own errors with a "humorous" quip designed to side-step personal accountability.

Let me see clearer how recklessness might be pushing me to make a joke at other's expense, or by "teasing" them to elevate myself, or even folding a half-disguised insult into a "light-hearted" comment.

Let your true humor in me shine through all such situations reflecting your perfection through me.

Let me not avoid your power to heal my _____ by clever jokes or crafty and deceiving comments meant only to divert my attention away from those things that I need to focus upon now.

Amen

Morning Prayer
Peace

I see the world clearer as I look through the lens of your peace.

Gracious Lord, I know that you've been watching over me the whole night through, and now your calm eyes greet me as I open mine to this day.

I see the world clearer as I look through the lens of your peace, and feel your celestial quiet saturating my heart with a sure calmness that only comes from you.

Harmony rests gently on me as your sacred tranquility innervates every crevice, fold, and juncture of my being.

Lord, help me experience your peace as we continue traveling on our mysterious and wonderful healing journey together today.

You are love itself, and I seek to live in that love.

Your peace is a portion of that love, Lord, and so I strive to seek out your peace today.

I needn't look far because you have tenderly planted your peace right in me; it purposefully patrols my being as a point of light seeking only to heal my _____.

Help me find peace today, Lord, and remain in it all day long.

Amen

Afternoon Prayer

Contention

The Shadow of Peace

Transform any of my oppositional tendencies into instruments for peace.

Oh Lord, my brokenness pushes me toward contention much too often.

Help me move to peace when I'm tempted to be defensive, or upset, or unfriendly, or contrary.

I don't wish these divisive reactions, Lord; of course I don't. Nonetheless, they show-up in my life just the same, driven by the murky inner shadow force of contention.

Your peace is the center of my soul and it's from this base of peace, this center point of peace, that I wish you to heal my _____ and all its consequences.

Lord, offer me the grace to convert my anger into a force for good and not become distorted in destruction.

Transform any of my oppositional tendencies into instruments for peace.

Lift any hint of defensiveness from me so I can see better who I am, and the fact that the real me needs no protection.

Help me Lord to grow beyond provoking contention in others or within myself, and instead sow peace.

Amen

Evening Prayer

Appeasement

The Compulsion of Peace

*Save me from placating or pacifying others,
fooling myself, and losing your peace.*

Lord, save me from making a "false peace" within my heart.

Help me see that my _____ needs your true and sacred healing, not a plastic or incomplete healing.

Let me dig into the depths of your peace where I know I will find the motivation to see clearly in your wholeness that resides there.

Help me shoulder the responsibility of making a true peace within me, with those around me, and with all my hurts as well.

Let me not falsely apologize or become overly promising.

Save me from placating or pacifying others and fooling myself; all of this only generates the false peace of appeasement.

Let me never abandon my true needs of moving only toward you.

You, Lord, are my only goal, my only quest in living.

Light up my healing with your grace, so I can see what needs to be done in the brightness of your peace.

Amen

Morning Prayer
Adaptability

Adaptability is essential for spiritual growth, without it I am doomed to remain the same.

How wonderful to awaken and view the world this morning in the new light of adaptability.

I luxuriate knowing that not only can I change, but also that you, Lord, expect me to change.

My only job today, as it is every day, is to learn how to love better than I did yesterday.

Learning how to love better requires your adaptability, Lord.

I am empowered by your gift of adaptability that allows me to shift my view as I grow in love.

Adaptability is essential for spiritual growth, without it I am doomed to the whims of my _____. You want and expect the opposite for and from me.

Adaptability propels me to see the light of God's ways operating in me, and so not to blindly take on the ways of the world.

I can learn God's will by seeing the fullness that is invested in me.

I can adjust myself toward you, Lord, I can be malleable in your hands; I can bend toward your ways and away from the ways of the world.

Amen

Afternoon Prayer

Rigidity

The Shadow of Adaptability

Lord, I long to see through your eyes of compassion, understanding, trust, and genuineness.

Lord, save me from the rigidity of sameness; save me from the threat of spiritual monotony.

You are alive in me and you call my deepest self to you.

I cannot be the same as I was yesterday and still grow toward you.

I need to change my perspective, and shift my point of view, so I can better align with yours.

Help me not cast a critical eye toward your creation, and help me not evaluate, but instead, help me fully experience your splendor in everything.

Lord, I long to see through your eyes of compassion, understanding, trust, and genuineness.

For all this, I lay myself at the feet of your grace of adaptability.

Help me take the logs out of my eyes and see my _____ clearer, see it as a teacher and not a tormentor.

Save me from stagnation and immobility and from being overly strict or harsh in my view of others and myself.

Amen

Evening Prayer
Self-Forfeiture
The Compulsion of Adaptability

Adaptability is my light this evening, the light of grace that illuminates me.

Oh happy evening! The shadows grow longer and I'm reminded of your magnificent gift of holy adaptability.

In its light, I can view my own needs as equally important to the needs of others. I do have the ability to say "no" to unnecessary tasks and demands.

Let me not forget that I do possess a sense of direction. I see that I am headed closer to my true self in you, Lord.

Help me not to be tempted or sidetracked by the idle cares and pseudo-needs of my ego or of others.

My views are valuable and I need to learn better how to express them in humility.

Adaptability is my light this evening, the point of light of grace that illuminates every corner of me with your power that heals my _____.

Sacred adaptability teaches me to discern and to trust my true perspective as a facet of your love, Lord.

I retain my integrity, my wholeness of spirit, by holding onto my true self.

Amen

Morning Prayer
Simplicity

I fully recognize the hand of God.

I marvel at the beauty of the morning light gracing the edge of my bed.

Today I awaken in exquisite sensitivity, like an infant touching her mother.

I see the morning light as beams of grace from above; I am enthralled by its majesty.

I fully recognize your healing hand touching me, Lord, soothing the pain of my _____.

I depend on your light, Lord, to bring me healing this day.

I see and appreciate the exquisite grandeur of this day as it dawns by your hand.

Today is sweet, uncomplicated, innocent, and without pretense — as am I also at my true core of grace.

Today is good; it possesses that divine quality of God that knows no bounds.

I experience this goodness and likewise know no boundaries today in appreciating the beautiful simplicity of the moment I now savor and want to keep in my heart all day long.

Amen

Afternoon Prayer

Complexity

The Shadow of Simplicity

Let my vision not be clouded by data and details that only serve to obscure your reality.

God, save me from my shadow of complexity.

Let the point of light that is your grace of simplicity, illuminate away that terrible darkness of complexity within me that bends my perception into distortion and stirs up my _____.

Help me remain vigilantly watchful for any overload or pressure that may upend my internal balance of grace.

Let my vision not be clouded by data and details that only serve to obscure your reality, Lord, and confound the simplicity I know to be true.

Save me from undue complications or entanglements that lure me toward the siren's song of complexity.

Lord, bring my hurts into the light of this day with its simple, childlike cheer; a cheer that you asked us to adopt as a sign of your love.

Save me from the paralysis that comes from excessive complexity, and grant me your simple yet profound ways of peace today.

Amen

Evening Prayer

Bluntedness

The Compulsion of Simplicity

I can become insensitive to the needs of others and blind to my own needs as well.

Without warning or awareness I can too often pervert my wondrous gift of simplicity and move toward bluntedness.

In this dark place I can further slip into an oversimplification that perverts my thinking away from your truth and toward an excessively narrow assessment of reality that can be far from the truth.

In this confined state I don't see the fullness of reality. I can become critical rather than appreciative, obtuse rather than approachable, and tactless rather than respectfully genuine.

I can too easily overlook the needs of others and blind to my own needs as well.

I can judge others and myself, heaping undeserved ridicule and prejudicial comments, which only blocks the flow of grace that can heal my _____ as well as my relationship with others.

Help me see a new day in a new way, a day when I can honor the simple truth without distorting it into something unreal

Lord, help me replace irreverence with respect and harsh views with your simple and beautiful ones.

Amen

Section Three

The Thinking Function

The Thinking Function

Thoughts are your almost automatic internal communications; they're like hundreds or maybe even thousands of internal e-mails flying around your mind at the same time each carrying bits of data. Some of these emails come from your perceiving function with data from the outside world, while others are internally produced by your thinking function. Through all this, it's hard to make sense of what's really going on and how to make sense of it. We need a filter.

You're thinking all the time, and the vast majority of that time you're quite unaware of what you're thinking. All these ideas are racing around your mind, each one charged with energy, and you're oblivious of them. Healing means that you become more aware of your thoughts: the ones that help you and the ones that don't (page 121, Discover Your Spiritual Strengths: Find Health, Healing & Happiness).

Morning Prayer

Faith

In the debris of my thoughts, I find solace on the solid rock of the grace of faith.

Something heavy pulls at my heart this morning as I raise my head off my pillow.

This unnamed intruder tugs at my mood dragging it down.

Where it came from is a mystery.

Amongst the debris of my fragmented thoughts, I find solace only on the solid rock of the grace of faith.

It's here in this place of fidelity where I know without question that your guiding hand brings me back to my center.

It's here where I stand on holy ground that settles my irritated mind and calms my thoughts.

You are my loyalty, Lord; you are my conviction; in you I find rest.

My _____ cannot overcome my faith; but it can strengthen my faith if I get out of the way and let your healing hands work, Lord.

The light of your grace of faith penetrates deep into every part of me, searching out any of my broken thoughts and replacing them with firmness and confidence.

Amen

Afternoon Prayer

Disloyalty

The Shadow of Faith

Pour out your grace of faith; illuminate my mind so I can think clearly again.

Oh, how my thoughts can twist my mind and cause me to resist you, Lord.

Help me to live by your precepts; help me to align my thoughts with yours; help me bend my knee as your faithful servant as you are so mystifyingly a servant for me.

Give me the grace of faith to collect my scattered thoughts, which divide and confuse my mind, pulling it away from you.

Help me bring my thoughts back to you.

Pour out your grace of faith; illuminate my mind so I can think clearly and accurately.

Enlighten my thinking so I can remain loyal to you and your teaching.

Extend to me, Lord, the grace of loyalty, the source of which is the only power strong enough to overcome my _____.

Help me find obedience so I can use your light of grace to overcome the darkness of my hurts and then discover your healing hand already on me.

Amen

Evening Prayer

Over-Zealousness

The Compulsion of Faith

Help me, Lord, to stay centered in you so that I don't get "carried-away" with thoughts.

Lord, help me tap into your strength so I can shift my near-obsessive thoughts back to you.

I seem unable to rid my mind of meaningless and self-centered thoughts that futilely focus on changing other people, the world, me, and even you, Lord.

I don't want compulsive thoughts; I want to be single-minded about you alone.

Help me, Lord, stay centered in and on you so that I don't get "carried-away" with my thoughts about changing what is unchangeable.

I am convicted about my thinking, but at times my conviction can extend beyond the borders of reason.

In a sense, I lose control of my thinking; my thinking begins controlling me rather than me controlling my thinking.

Help me find your true faith, Lord, and in this power from you I know I will find healing of my _____.

Help me center on the point of light of faith that you have planted in me from my conception.

Amen

Morning Prayer

Wisdom

Let me join my mind with your mind, Lord.

Lord, animate me with your wisdom all day long.

Saturate my thoughts with your highest purpose.

Allow me to let go of all unnecessary thoughts that only clutter my mind and bring it to insufficiency.

Let me use the knowledge that flows from you as the basis for my thinking all day, Lord.

Let me discover and use the most illuminated, enlightened, enriching thoughts ...your thoughts, so that I can discern the "right meaning" from the events and relationships of this day.

Let me join my mind with your mind, so that in this sublime alignment I can find your uplifting unity of thought that gives me confidence, good cheer, and healing of my _____ all day long.

Let me properly discern your wisdom in ways that allow me to walk straight and solid with you all day long.

Help me embrace your light, overcome my dread of darkness, and find my healing path to you.

Amen

Afternoon Prayer

Inadequacy

The Shadow of Wisdom

Clear away my cloudy and folly-filled thinking.

Lord, allow the brightness of your wisdom to eradicate any distrust of myself that I may harbor in my mind.

Through your grace, let me surmount any thoughts of being "not good enough."

Unravel my persistent thoughts of personal inferiority, Lord.

Grant me reprieve from the inaccurate ways I can denigrate and hurt myself.

With your holy light, clear away my cloudy and folly-filled thinking and replace these tendencies with your grace of wisdom.

Help me more fully accept your wisdom and let its truth wash over me and cleanse my soul.

Allow me to join my thoughts with your thoughts, and in this marvelous and loving synthesis, discover your healing for my _____.

Amen

Evening Prayer

Perfectionism

The Compulsion of Wisdom

Save me from my perverted "need" for ever-greater accomplishment.

Lord, let me ask that you reinforce the strength of wisdom that you've already given to me.

I firmly think that you and I together can overcome any compulsion of chronic dissatisfaction I have with my accomplishments, as well as those unrealistic demands I sometimes place on myself and others.

Lift my thoughts beyond any adolescent need to always be right.

Save me from any twisted "need" for ever-more accomplishment, and internal demands for ever-increasing productivity.

Grant me the wisdom, Lord, so I can loosen any distorted tendencies of continuously raising my standards ever higher, tendencies that can keep me in turmoil and only aggravate my

_____.

Finally, Lord, allow me to gather the light from your wisdom so that I may more fully accept your grace.

Your wisdom is the only power that frees me from the sadness and anxiety that still seems to cling to me in the many forms that perfectionism can take.

Amen

Morning Prayer
Steadfastness

I find my firmness and determination only in you.

Lord, you are my anchor.

I open myself to the world today and know that you are with me forever. What better thought can there be than this?

You fix me in place, but I am not stuck; rather this kind of "fixing" paradoxically allows me a new freedom to think with the surety of love and the confidence of your Spirit, the wellspring of all grace.

I move only in you dear, Lord, and while I move closer to you, I also know that this movement brings me to the center of all healing, the site of all power and might.

Healing only comes from, and is only found in you, Lord. I find my firmness and determination only in you.

You are unfaltering, and by extension, because of your gift of steadfastness, I can find a secure path of healing in you.

My _____ can never negate the utter dependability and constancy that comes only from you, when I am in sync with your steadfastness.

Your light of purposefulness brightens my soul and brings me to the gates of healing.

In you I am sure.

Amen

Afternoon Prayer

Unreliable

The Shadow of Steadfastness

I need your light of grace, the grace of steadfastness to show me the way.

How can I escape my shadow of unreliability?

I am ashamed to admit any lack of self-discipline.

I need your help, Lord, to address those times when I can make excuses for what I have failed to do, those times when I hide behind my defensiveness, and even laziness.

I'm overly sensitive to any unreliability that I sense in others; while at the same time I'm blind to it in myself.

My shadow isn't always apparent to me; I can hide it with all my strength because it stands in stark contrast to how I want to see myself.

I so want to be dependable, but I need your light of grace, the grace of steadfastness, to heal my _____.

Help me accept the limits of my capabilities, and save me from all the ways I unknowingly show my unreliability.

Help me shape my thoughts away from irresponsibility, especially any irresponsibility that I previously repressed into unawareness, and toward you, Lord.

Amen

Evening Prayer

Fixated

The Compulsion of Steadfastness

Let not my hurt become a further fixation confounding my search for you.

Lord, help me extract my thoughts from the quicksand of becoming fixated. I can sometimes become so pre-occupied with meaningless thoughts that I fail to see what is real.

Too easily I avoid even necessary life modifications; I need your light of grace to open my darkened mind.

Help me align my thoughts with your thoughts so I can grow toward you. Help me develop according to your plan, not mine.

Heal my _____ Lord, and in the new freedom it gives I can better find my way to you. Help me become clear headed and as free from worldly constraint as possible so I can become more like you, Lord.

Unlock my stubborn thoughts and help me replace them with an eagerness of heart and a vitality of mind.

Help me find steadfastness so I can rid my mind of compulsive thoughts that stagnate me and prevent my healing of my

_____ .

Let me stand shoulder-to-shoulder with your hurting children and find my path to constructive conversion.

Amen

Morning Prayer
Wholeness

Lord, let wholeness be the point of light today that guides me to your love.

Good morning, Lord, I come to you today to do your will.

My job today is nothing short of bringing your love to my little corner of the world.

I desire nothing more than to live in your love; today that means living in your holy grace of wholeness.

Lord, let wholeness be the point of light that guides me to you today.

Your wholeness, which you send to me in a channel of grace, is the power that can heal my _____.

I know that your presence in my mind is divine: intact, complete, and unbroken, yet I live in a world that lacks these things.

Today, with your assistance, I again regroup my thoughts and concentrate only on my one authentic goal of living, your universal love.

I seek mental coherence, bringing all my disparate thoughts together into an integrated whole, into you.

I know that the only perfect wholeness is in you Lord.

Today I seek your holy wholeness, that sacred state of personality integration.

Amen

Afternoon Prayer

Fragmented

The Shadow of Wholeness

I long to become whole; my thoughts full and undivided.

I am broken; part of my woundedness is my vulnerability to fragmentation of thought.

This shadow of fragmentation causes insecurity to break through the otherwise still surface of my conscious mind and disrupt my thoughts; at times this insecurity grows into stress and/or strain, and even anxiety.

At times I can even feel mentally scattered, like my thoughts are simply disconnected pieces floating around aimlessly.

I want to melt into your grace-power of wholeness, Lord; I long to become whole, with my thoughts full, developed, and undivided.

I need your grace to live in the tension caused by my fear of becoming disconnected from myself and from you.

I ask for the grace of your wholeness to calm my mind, to give me the strength to find coherence in a disconnected world, and give me healing of my _____.

I visualize your light of wholeness illuminating my mind and making it whole, bringing together all my confused thinking, and giving me peace.

Amen

Evening Prayer

Provincial

The Compulsion of Wholeness

Help me elevate my thinking and be more mindful of living in your presence.

Help me expand my thinking today, Lord; help me transform my dull thoughts into ones that sparkle with your wholeness.

By your grace, save me from thinking thoughts that are too narrow, too shallow, and too constricted.

Help me broaden my thinking. Too often my thinking focuses only on the insignificant and meaningless details of daily living.

My thoughts are so often stuck on the tangible plane where confusion reigns; help me transform my thinking to focus on you, Lord.

Without thoughts of you, my mind remains in turmoil, a turmoil that blocks your healing grace of wholeness from finding its intended mark on my _____.

Help me elevate my thinking and be ever more mindful of placing myself in the light of your presence more consistently.

When I think so small, I miss your magnificence and I overlook your grandeur, this blocks me from living in your love, and from being "in love." I want to find your awe, wonder, and delight that I know is there but which so often escapes me.

Amen

Morning Prayer

Charity

Let me discover your charity today, Lord, to give and expect nothing in return.

I awaken thinking of you, Lord, and how you shower me with abundance.

Charity reminds me this morning that this abundance is not just all the giftedness that I think of as "good," but all the rest as well, including all those things, relationships, events, happenings, and thoughts that I formerly considered quite the opposite of good.

All of this is part of your abundance as well.

Help me today, Lord, by your unconditional benevolent goodwill of charity to accept every part of your abundance.

This includes all the parts that I like, as well as my _____, which I didn't choose, but which I know can in some mysterious way encourage my journey to you.

Everything is part of your abundance.

Let me discover your charity today, Lord: to give and expect nothing in return; to help others selflessly; and to recognize other's needs and give generously to them.

Send me your strength of charity today so that I can learn how to love better by shedding any encumbrances that have prevented me from living fully in you.

Amen

Afternoon Prayer

Judgmental

The Shadow of Charity

I need your goodwill, Lord, to save me from chronic criticism.

When I forget my spiritual strength of charity, I drift toward a fearsome coastline that eventually leaves me shipwrecked on the rocks of cynical and negative thinking.

In this cold and barren land I can become opinionated, malevolent, and ill-tempered of thought toward others, toward myself, and even toward you, Lord.

I need your goodwill, Lord, to save me from this chronic criticism, acrimony, and incessant judgment.

My inner critic works overtime searching the horizon for any bits of data that it can convert into negatives; it bites at the heels of my mind with a vengeance.

Such thinking robs me of the generosity of charity and keeps me cognitively confined to a rancorous resentfulness that sucks your power and might right out of me.

Help me, Lord, to re-establish connection with charity so I can capture your grace, the light inside that can heal my _____, so I can once again find real life in you.

Amen

Evening Prayer

Servitude

The Compulsion of Charity

Let me submit my thoughts only to you, Lord.

Lord, I thank you for the power of charity that helps me give of myself in a selfless manner. Charity beckons me to submit myself to do your work here on this plane by giving freely to others.

But Lord, help me not submit my thinking to anything else but you. By the power of charity, help me retain ownership of my thinking and not forfeit it in blind submission to any person or force that is not you and thereby cause my _____ to threaten me more.

Help me hold fast onto my freedom of thought and not lose my liberty of using my mind in your service.

I am your servant only, Lord; by charity, save me from any slavish devotion to another's wishes that may hinder my journey with you.

Save my mind from becoming twisted or confused by some distorted conformity to this world.

Give me the strength of charity so that worldly forces don't capture my thinking and make my mind their prisoner.

Let me submit my thoughts only to you, Lord.

Amen

Section Four

The Feeling Function

The Feeling Function

Feelings are the automatic consequence of your thoughts; every thought, or thought bundle, immediately generates a feeling or bundle of feelings. Interestingly, you have the least volitional influence over your personality feeling function than you do of any of the other five functions. However, you do have immense influence over to what degree and how long a feeling takes up residence in you.

So much of our overall emotional health is determined by our feelings, because our feelings determine our mood more than any other personality force. When we feel 'good,' we're generally in a positive mood, and of course we all know that the opposite is true as well. We've all had down days, sad times, a sour disposition, and a dour temperament at times. Depression, chronic or cyclical feelings of sadness, anger, irritability or just plain melancholia, seems part of the fabric of our lives (page 148, <u>Discover Your Spiritual Strengths: Find Health, Healing & Happiness</u>).

Morning Prayer
Joyfulness

I am filled with awe and wonder; I'm bursting with your joy.

Oh happy day, you Lord are here with me still, standing straight and tall at my center.

Let me find your holy delight today, Lord. I wish to live fully in your happiness of heart.

I am jubilant all day, feeling your love as my only reality and my only work today.

Your grace of joy sustains me today, and sends my heart into a free-spirited elation.

I am so filled with awe and wonder that I can hardly contain myself; I'm bursting with your joy.

Even when this world weighs heavily upon me, even when it pushes and prods me, attacks me, and disappoints me; even in these dark times, my heart remains joyful knowing that you alone heal my _____.

Joyfulness is your holy light in me that leads me away from emotional turmoil and toward your calm healing waters.

Joy conquers sorrow by lifting my spirits up beyond the cares of this world and resting them gently on you.

Amen

Afternoon Prayer

Dejection

The Shadow of Joyfulness

I feel dejected at times, but I cannot be dejected because I can only be with you.

Save me from sadness of heart and spirit Lord; instead of sadness, I accept your fullness of heart by your power of joy.

When I find myself emotionally flat, perk me up with your effervescent joy. I submerse myself in your pool of joy that washes any dreary feelings away; I emerge fully cleansed of heart and soul with my _____ healed.

Your joy dislodges my scales of gloom and dismay; they slide from my shoulders giving me spirited relief and healing.

Your light pushes out all dark brooding, sulking, and dismal feelings and gradually brings me back to my center, back to joy.

Even in the midst of these dark days I can still feel joy knowing that you never leave me, you never abandon me. Lord, you carry me on your shoulders over my toughest times.

I feel dejected at times, but I cannot be dejected because I can only be with you.

Even when I walk the edges of depression, you are there with me holding a lantern that gives me direction and warms my heart.

Amen

Evening Prayer

Hyperphoria

The Compulsion of Joyfulness

*Help me confront the low times, which may
have much to teach me.*

At times I fear losing control of my feelings, like a roller coaster about to fly off the tracks.

With the power of true joy, help me turn away from the compulsion to slide into excessive exuberance that sometimes seems to take over my heart.

Help me realize that I need the calm of being centered; help me regain my heart's true desire and not always yearn for a rush of energy.

True interior joy calms my mood so I can once again return to you at my center.

Help me confront the low times, which may have much to teach me, and not try to flee from them into any excessiveness.

Slow me down, Lord, and give me your power to be more intentional with my feelings and not throw caution to the wind.

Your light of joy can heal my _____ that sometimes threatens to sweep me away into an illusionary place where I lose my bearings, because you're not there, Lord.

Amen

Morning Prayer

Trust

Today I wish to fall into you because you are enough for all my needs today, Lord.

I open my eyes this morning confident of your care all day long.

The strength of my feelings for you, Lord, moves me beyond mere belief in your love for me all the way to an assured knowing of your love for me.

Today, I trust.

Thank you for illuminating my emotions out of the darkness of seeking security in this world, a place where there is no certainty, to the only true security, which exists in you.

Today I wish to fall into you because you are the abundant provider. You are both necessary and sufficient for all my needs today, Lord.

I cannot trust in me or in anything else; I can only trust in you. There are no guarantees except you, Lord.

Your universal love is my sure light that penetrates through any darkness and heals my _____.

I have no doubt that your promise of abundance is being fulfilled even now, as always.

In absolute assurance, I give my life over to you forever.

Amen

Afternoon Prayer

Insecurity

The Shadow of Trust

Let me find your light of assurance, the light that envelops me and heals my illness.

Lord, by your holy trust save me from the times when I'm emotionally shaky, times when I feel unfastened and free-floating, with nothing to hold onto.

Lord, help me find your stability when I feel so unstable, as though I stand on quaking ground.

Lord, help me reach for your hand when I feel all confidence draining from me. I search for some surety, a solid place where I can escape feeling so vulnerable and unprotected.

Let me find your light of assurance Lord, the light that envelops me and heals my _____.

Save me, Lord, from the pangs and fears of anxiety that squeezes whatever meager resolve I possess right out of me.

I can feel so inept when I lose heart; my confidence slips from me, and my determination departs. You are my security, Lord.

At times like these I feel like running away from life, hiding from the terrible critique that I fear lurks around every corner.

Lord, help me always remember that you are my sure refuge and my solid strength.

Amen

Evening Prayer

Reductionism

The Compulsion of Trust

Lord, help me trust your voice within me.

Lord, help me stay steady in your trust.

Let me not reduce your trust into adolescent formulas and simplistic solutions for living my life.

Let me keep rules and regulations in proper perspective and not pervert them into inflated demands for perfection, only shallow substitutes for trust in you.

Redirect my vulnerability toward seeking black-and-white answers to questions; you cannot be reduced to a duality. You Lord are the fullness of space and time, the Alpha and the Omega.

Help me not slide into always wanting outside authority to lead my heart; instead, help me trust your voice within me.

Help me capture the power and might of trust that opens up my feelings so I can embrace constructive change and not always look to past solutions as the superior answer to questions of my heart.

Help me look forward to the newness of you and not only to the past where tired and worn-out answers cannot satisfy me today.

Lord, you heal my _____ with simple love, not simplistic fear.

Amen

Morning Prayer
Love-Finder

I feel your love all around me.

Love is everywhere this morning, and my job today is to find it.

I look only for the true reality of you, Lord.

I seek the majesty of your awe, the mystery of your wonder, and the magnificence of your delight today.

The power and beauty of your love gives everything, both inside and outside of me, a sparkling patina that reflects your indwelling presence.

I feel your love all around me, under me, above me, beside me, in front of me, and behind me.

I am surrounded by love and innervated by love.

Help me detect your love in everyone I meet today; let me see you in their eyes, hear your voice in them, and discern the glow of their saintly light.

I am drawn to your light of love as it gently touches every part of me, healing my _____.

I plunge into your love today, and I feel refreshed.

Amen

Afternoon Prayer

Fault-Seeker

The Shadow of Love-Finder

Help me beyond my penchant toward being critical and negativistic.

Lord, help me look away from all the blemishes that I find in myself and others.

Let your strength beckon me away from focusing on defects and imperfections and instead focus on your love reflected on this beautiful, yet imperfect earthly plane.

Help me look past the folly and foibles of this world to the freedom and fascination of your love where I find healing for my
_____.

Help me over my penchant toward being sometimes critical and negativistic. Forgive me when I'm sarcastic and sneering.

Instead, allow me to feel the warmth of your light of health, healing, and holiness.

Let me give up my distorted dualistic expectations and realize that I don't need to be superlative to escape my critique of being a failure.

Your strength of love-finding lights my way over the dark bridge of pettiness and pessimism to your bright land of loving where I can release the weight of anger.

Amen

Evening Prayer

Pollyannaism

The Compulsion of Love-Finder

I cannot turn my back on the world that needs my strength.

While love is everywhere, I am still in this world and need to recognize its basic brokenness. I can neither overlook the pain of strife nor the bleakness of sin that is folded into the fabric of the human condition.

Help me not disregard the fact that shadows and compulsions can spin out of control and cause unmeasured damage in every life circumstance.

I cannot turn my back on the world that needs my strength. I cannot exclude, reject, or overlook the callousness and even horror of human action where it rejects your love, Lord.

Help me get past my compulsion to become so overly optimistic that I completely miss your healing of my _____.

Help me respond to your call by first taking off my rose-colored glasses that can at times blind me to the needs of others.

I see the love that is everywhere, but I also feel the degradation of the human soul caused by brutality, greed, and pride.

I accept the challenge of your love to use my strengths not just for my own betterment but also for the good of all.

Amen

Morning Prayer

Empathy

Let me be exquisitely sensitive to the needs of others and to my own needs as well.

Lord, grant me the strength of empathy today.

Allow me access to your beautiful sensitivity of heart so that I might be fully present to your children in their deepest need.

Let me bear the heartache of others even when the pain threatens to disrupt me.

Let me be exquisitely sensitive to the needs of others and not forget my own needs as well.

Let me be moved by distress, touched by tragedy, and affected by the woundedness in this world.

Yet, also Lord, let me celebrate in your good news, delight in the joys of others, and stand in awe of your wonder that I might otherwise overlook. This is, after all a beautiful world still.

Allow me to open my heart and be thoroughly accepting of your healing touch on my _____.

Let me be devout in honoring all feelings as reminders of the goodness that I know, without question, throbs in the hearts of all your children.

Amen

Afternoon Prayer

Obtuseness

The Shadow of Empathy

Let me always be emotionally intuitive.

Lord, help me surmount all my vulnerabilities toward insensitivity.

Let me emotionally engage with others and not remain impassive; offer a warm not a cold heart; and render a soft not a callous touch.

As the shadows get longer in the late afternoon, let me not forget to offer these life-giving sensitivities to myself as well.

I have hardened my heart to myself too often and have suffered the sting of self-rebuke, instead of the balm of consolation.

Let me not avoid the reality of my emotions or those of others.

Emotions possess your power, Lord; help me value them even in the stressed and wounded state I find myself.

Let me open more fully to your strength of empathy in me and find the true power of your emotional intelligence that is resident therein, Lord.

Let me be emotionally intuitive so I can freely embrace your power and your will to heal my _____.

Amen

Evening Prayer

Ingratiating

The Compulsion of Empathy

I need to place this compulsion of always needing praise from others on your altar of healing.

Lord, help me overcome my tendency to contort myself to gain another's favor. Help me become more aware of the times, places, and people when, where, and whom I subject to this unfortunate tendency.

My exaggerated need to be liked can be so strong that I submerge my true self and show only what I feel others want from me. I fear that I am sometimes like a chameleon changing "colors" not to fade into the background, but to stand out or be liked.

I can over-depend on others for feeling good about myself. Help me to find true joy in you and you alone. My heart breaks when I recognize this vulnerability at work in me, but even this compulsion I need to place on your altar of healing so I can remain in touch with the true self you have created in me.

Lord, I need the grace of your true empathy; I know you have planted it in me to heal my _____.

I know I do not need to do anything to win your acceptance, Lord. But help me to seek only your love, which will wash over me and cleanse my _____.

Amen

Morning Prayer

Gratitude

The light of gratitude pulsates in praise as it makes its rounds through me.

I awaken in profound thankfulness for another day, Lord.

I bow my head and bend my knee; without you I can do nothing.

My very personality is animated only by your power and your gifts, Lord.

Today is a day of 'thank you,' a day of tribute to you.

The light of gratitude pulsates in praise as it makes its rounds through me —searching for and eliminating any misguided emotions that could pull me away from you.

Let me always remember how indebted I am to you, Lord; you know all about me and know particularly what I need now in my life.

I stand in reverence this morning basking in your overwhelming abundance.

I so appreciate your light of gratitude as it penetrates into my _____ like a benevolent laser beam activating healing.

I praise your name all the days of my life...forever.

Amen

Afternoon Prayer

Blaming

The Shadow of Gratitude

Lord, help me get past my ridiculing heart.

Lord, why is it so easy for me to feel blame and also to place blame on others?

What is this confusing hold that blame has upon me?

Sometimes I can be so pointed in my speech; at other times I have to fight to keep my condemning attitude at bay.

I don't see myself as critical; I'm actually overly sensitive to critique from others, and yet I'm strangely drawn to participate in blame mostly in my own heart, but sometimes even publicly.

I don't understand this paradox Lord, yet I invite your healing grace of gratitude into my _____.

I ask for your light of healing that alone can warm me with forgiveness and peace.

I reprove myself for being even slightly invested in blame, both at myself and at others.

Lord, grant me the gratitude to get past my ridiculing heart, help me beyond my biting thoughts and feelings, and return me to my center point in you.

Amen

Evening Prayer

Submissiveness

The Compulsion of Gratitude

Help me stand as tall as you made me and not sink into fawning submissiveness.

Help me be grateful, Lord, for all that you have given me, rather than so diminishing of these gifts even to the point of denying them. I put myself 'down' without ever realizing it at all.

Help me stand as tall as I can, as tall as you made me, and not sink into fawning submissiveness.

My emotions automatically put others ahead of me, as though they were somehow better than I am.

Sometimes I can feel emotionally paralyzed by a sense of inferiority that I know in my heart isn't true, and yet it paces like a caged tiger in me. I feel your grace of gratitude as it isolates my _____ and eradicates it.

Lord, I ask your help in moving from the emptiness of submissiveness to the fullness of your grace of true gratitude.

Help me move beyond a dispiriting feeling that I should somehow apologize for my vague feelings of unworthiness.

Help me get past my illusionary over-attempts to be as good as I see others as being, and divert these feelings of chronic unworthiness to my advancing journey with you.

Amen

Section Five

The Deciding Function

The Deciding Function

It's been said that life (and healing) is a series of decisions, decisions, and more decisions. Making decisions can be perplexing. Yet making decisions is not an option if you want to live fully and find healing.

Healing requires strength, and strength is derived from personal power. All change, especially change required for healing and spiritual deepening, requires an attitude of surrender to the power of the Most High. Surrender requires a decision. Healing demands self-control and self-discipline, all ingredients of the deciding function of your personality. Decisions position you so that positive healing can become a working reality in your life.

We all have personal power; the question is to what degree have we tapped into our own personal power by making prudent choices...making decisions for healing (page 179, <u>Discover Your Spiritual Strengths: Find Health, Healing & Happiness</u>)?

Morning Prayer

Harmony

Help me shape my goals so they all point to living in sync with you.

This morning holds every promise.

As I open my eyes I encounter you first, Lord.

The advancing light creates an eager readiness in me to receive you anew.

My awakening consciousness reminds me that my only agenda today is to be in harmony with you alone.

You are my companion all day long; your light guides me and heals my _____.

Help me find solace in your harmony as the central principle of my life.

Give me the internal harmony so peace can grow verdantly in the sacred garden at my core.

Help me shape my goals so they all point to living in sync with you.

You are the cohesiveness of my heart and the glue holding my will together.

Harmony creates the strong bond that keeps me close to you and helps me take on your goals as my own.

Amen

Afternoon Prayer

Chaos

The Shadow of Harmony

I know that true order comes only from you; I wish to surrender to your order.

Sometimes I feel like I'm coming apart.

I feel chaotic when I have no solid goals, when I lack direction, and when my purpose is confused.

Save me, with your strength of harmony, from my tendencies toward internal disorder, disorganization, and clutter of soul.

My life needs order, Lord; I know that ultimate order comes only from you, and I so sorely wish to surrender to your order.

Sometimes I can feel so fragmented…a free-floating anxiety that my life could fall into pieces; I even fear that sometimes it already has, and I haven't been paying attention.

I need to "get my head together," to find my center in, you Lord.

I need to be grounded in you, to find my stability and security in you, Lord, the wellspring of harmony.

Help me find integrity of body, clarity of mind, and solidity of spirit, so that with the power of your grace I can surrender this terrible confusion, which I feel inside me, over to you—the only one strong enough and big enough to take it in and heal my

_____.

Amen

Evening Prayer

Equivocation

The Compulsion of Harmony

My overheated conscientiousness prevents me from finding harmony in you.

Lord, save me from the paralysis of personal doubt, the pain of somehow feeling that I will fail. I know I can't fail when my decisions reflect your will for me.

Relieve my endless hesitation of will, trying to decide the absolute "right" course of action. I know you are the only course I want to follow. My overheated conscientiousness can keep me in turmoil and prevent me from finding harmony in you.

Help me get beyond the terrible tendency to always "keep my options open" and hence never find a solid place to make a genuine and complete commitment to you.

I know that this confusion of indecision blocks your healing efforts of my _____.

I fear making the wrong decision and so I find myself trying to avoid making any decisions at all.

Sometimes I try to please everyone, seeking harmony for all. Of course this kind of harmony is impossible...yet I strive for it.

Lord, pull me away from trying to do too much in a frantic effort to satisfy everyone.

Amen

Morning Prayer
Patience

I calmly continue in you, Lord, whatever the adversity or hardship.

Good morning, Lord. My only goal today is to tap into the mysterious calm of your creation, to listen to the middle "C" note of your immense universe in perfect pitch.

Today I wait only in your time not my time.

I long to live at my serene center point. There is the only place where I can find true composure.

Lord, help me become ever more mindful of the "process" of living rather than becoming frustrated with the "product" of living.

I calmly continue in you, Lord, whatever adversity or hardship, whatever difficulties, or whatever distractions may befall me.

I long to enter into, and remain in, that still point of your tranquility today, regardless of the gongs and sirens, flashing lights, and pandering calls that I may encounter.

I calmly keep my sight firmly affixed on your steady and sure light of patience, where I find the direction that illuminates my soul and shrinks my _____.

Amen

Afternoon Prayer

Impulsivity

The Shadow of Patience

Healing occurs in your time Lord; I cannot force it no matter what I do.

The world wants decision and action "right now."

Help me, Lord, with your patience, to live in your NOW, your ever-immediate love, and not be pushed from my center by a demanding world.

I know I must live in the linear time of the material world, but help me avoid being so captivated by the impulsiveness of the world marketplace that I forget that it's only in your eternal time that I find my real life.

Healing occurs in your time Lord; I cannot force it, no matter what I do.

Help me step back, Lord, and let go of my time-stressed goals; help me move away from my unrealistic agenda and let your Spirit heal my _____.

Stepping back, letting-go, and moving away from impulsivity are my healing choices today.

With the strength of your patience, I can respond rather than react; I can thoughtfully consider rather than hastily jump in.

I patiently commit to your plan, Lord, and give over my own.

Amen

Evening Prayer

Unresponsiveness

The Compulsion of Patience

Lord, give me the patience to make the decisions I must.

Patience is one of your gifts to me, but, Lord, sometimes I can pervert your wondrous gift.

Save me, Lord, from over-doing patience to the point of becoming unresponsive to your will. I can sometimes slip into a sluggishness of mind and action and an indolence of decision.

At these times I place my life on hold, I don't make decisions; it's like I'm numb to my needs and the needs of others (especially those close to me).

Lord, help me focus on what you're asking of me ...I sometimes can become deaf to the decisions I need to make.

Lord, give me the patience to break through my unresponsiveness and make the decisions I must.

Sometimes I can be simply lazy; sometimes I don't want to disrupt my comfortable lifestyle; sometimes I just want to remain in my "own world," while at other times I'm just confused.

Compulsions like these block you from healing my _____ and hinder my growth in your Spirit.

Help me with your patience.

Amen

Morning Prayer

Strength

Your strength is the potent grace that illuminates my soul and brings blessed healing.

I look around my life this morning and realize that you are my only direction, Lord; you are the sole fountain of strength.

I so need your strength, Lord; I rely on you for the fortitude to keep going, for the power and might that alone can heal my

_____.

Your strength is that point of light and grace that illuminates my soul and brings blessed healing.

I always want to keep you as my primary goal. Your strength is my power for the constructive change of healing, for transformation of my soul that sorely needs healing.

Your strength animates me; it gives me solace knowing that nothing can truly harm me when I live in your strength, Lord.

Today help me clarify my goals so I can walk a straight path in your strength.

I need your strength to pull me through, to give me direction, to provide me with a plan that will sustain me especially during this difficult time.

Lord, grant me the capacity for sustained exertion ...only in your strength.

Amen

Afternoon Prayer

Impotence

The Shadow of Strength

I can sometimes feel so rudderless and incapable, so incompetent and insufficient.

Lord, I am weak; without you I lack the stamina to carry on.

Grant me your strength to overcome the horrid powerlessness that overtakes me at times, robbing me of my resolve and morale, and stripping me of trust in you.

I seem so often overcome by fear and doubt, I fear I lack the necessary determination and volition to surrender to your holy healing of my _____.

I lack the strategies for healing; I see no options for escaping from this vortex of fear that threatens to pull me under.

I can sometimes feel so rudderless and incapable, so incompetent and insufficient.

I know this is all groundless, yet I fall prey to the viciousness of the shadow of impotence, and feel that I have nowhere to turn.

Help me always turn to you, Lord. Send your light of strength to illuminate my capacity to grow beyond exhaustion, beyond demoralization, and beyond paralysis of spirit.

Amen

Evening Prayer

Brutishness

The Compulsion of Strength

Help me make the choices that you would make Lord.

Sometimes I can make such stupid choices.

When I'm pressed by fear or frustration and/or pushed by pain or loss, I can, without even being aware of it, become heavy-handed with others and with myself.

I can become short, indelicate, and even terse in my responses.

Help me make the choices that you would make, Lord. Sometimes my choices lack true consideration for all concerned; they can be self-serving, blunt, and even hurtful.

My intentions are not malicious, rather I fear appearing weak; I try to over-compensate by merely appearing strong, but I can overdo it.

Save me from any tendencies toward brutishness, Lord, in whatever forms it may take.

Help me align my will with your will; I know that you want the best for me.

I pray that you shore me up with your grace of strength so that I can accept your healing of my _____.

Amen

Morning Prayer
Transcendence

Today I move beyond the realm of simply "doing" and enter the realm of "being."

As I awaken from my slumber, I ask you, Lord, to show me the mystical ways of transcendence; that I am, at one and the same time, both <u>in</u> this world but I am not <u>of</u> this world.

Healing requires that I join with you in making decisions from the highest reality, from your reality, Lord, the most real reality there is.

Today I move beyond the realm of simply "doing" and enter the realm of "being."

Lord, today I long to be both "in" and "of" you. You are the only sure path leading to healing of my _____.

I want to join my will with your will, Lord; this requires that I live fully in both the material world and the spiritual realm at the same time.

As I do, I find that I become fundamentally changed. I am transformed. You bring me beyond the material and invite me to begin walking the outer lawns of your numinous plane.

I am both here on this earth and also with you at the same time.

Your transcendence causes a core shift in me, a shift toward you.

Amen

Afternoon Prayer

Worldliness

The Shadow of Transcendence

Help me make decisions not as the world makes them, but as you make them.

Lord, help me sever the pull that this world has on me; help me move away from living only in this world, being a citizen of this world only, and seeing my roles and personal definition only as the world sees me...and no more.

I know that I am so much more than what the world says that I am. I am your child first and foremost.

Let me decide to break free of the way the world sees me and instead choose the option of seeing myself as you view me.

Help me make the commitment to invite your healing power into my _____ by making decisions not as the world would make them, but as you would make them.

When I come to a fork in the road and must decide which one to take, help me use your strength of transcendence in me to choose the path that you would have me take.

I can be so mindlessly dazzled and thoughtlessly confused by the world and what it has to offer, to such a degree that I'm blinded to the treasures that you offer.

Help me keep my halo straight today, Lord.

Amen

Evening Prayer

Unreality

The Compulsion of Transcendence

Help me find myself again in the truest reality... your reality.

Stir up my strength of transcendence, Lord, and save me from constructing fantasies and illusions.

With little or no awareness of the process I use, nor the fantasies I create, I find myself wanting things, relationships, events, and miracles that lack your rational sense and order.

Let me see the true reality of love as my standard for making decisions.

Let me move beyond my illusionary expectations that create unreality and grab onto the solid and sure handhold that you offer me, Lord.

Free me from making unrealistic commitments that I cannot keep.

Lead me away from fantasies, Lord. Help me stay centered in your transcendence and there discover your power to heal my _____.

Keep me away from the land of unreality where I'm blinded to the true discernment of spirit that comes only from you.

Help me find myself again in the truest reality... your reality.

Amen

Morning Prayer
Self-Discipline

I pray that I may have the power to focus only on your point of light of self-discipline.

This morning I decide to truly surrender my ego, my worldly self, over to you. In so doing, I open myself up to your divine direction.

I seek to be obedient only to you, Lord.

My ego-self wants me to choose the siren's song and pandering voice of the world. I know this brings me only separation from you and causes my hurts to flourish.

Help me be in allegiance with you first, Lord. Help me seek you first and place your will for me as the true north of my being.

I pray that I may have the power to accept your point of light of self-discipline and embrace your healing of my _____.

Help me to seek your grace of self-discipline alone, rather than circling the drain of self-indulgence.

You create the splendor in me, Lord, and through your power of self-discipline in me, you allow me to achieve new heights of wholeness otherwise unattainable.

Amen

Afternoon Prayer

Self-Indulgence

The Shadow of Self-Discipline

Bring order to my mind, calmness to my heart, and determination to my will.

Lord, I can falter. I can too easily be swept up in the whirlwind of the bling and tinsel of the world.

Help me say "no" to those nagging forces of inertia that bite at my resolve; help me follow you more nearly.

Help me open to your divine discipline Lord; I know that it can heal my _____.

Help me wipe laziness, idleness, and inactivity from me. Lord, guide me away from my dolt-like lack of self-control.

Bring order to my mind, resolve to my heart, and determination to my will.

Help me see when enough is enough, and that I needn't yearn for more.

Help me be satisfied in you and turn away from the enticing excesses that my ego desires.

I ask for your mighty grace of self-discipline so I can get a firmer grip on my inner-urges that can move off my center.

In you I trust, Lord.

Amen

Evening Prayer

Self-Repression

The Compulsion of Self-Discipline

Help me recognize that this senseless self-control is not your will for me.

Lord, while I can sometimes be self-indulgent, at other times I can pervert your grace of self-discipline and cross over into self-repression.

This, of course, is not my intention, but nonetheless by some distortion of desire, I give myself too many "shoulds."

I can, at times, demand too much from me, I push for unattainable achievement; I impose stricture on my self that defies reason and constricts me.

Lord, free me from this self-imposed drive where I demand more and more of me with relentless disregard for balance.

Help me recognize that this excessive self-control is not your will for me, but only my contorted desire to hold down the terrible fear of failure that sometimes infects my soul.

I need your light of self-discipline to release me from my own self-suppression of will, a repression that blocks your healing from my

_____.

I want to find the freedom of your will for me. May thy will and not my will be done, Lord.

Amen

Section Six

The Acting Function

The Acting Function

All of creation, all that we can see, and the utter vastness of what we can't see, is the result of the action of a powerful hand. The elegantly swirling galaxies, the incomprehensible distance of space, the vibrancy and tenderness of the star nurseries, the terrible power of black holes, and the dazzle of the seas of stars, all bespeak a wonder of divine action so gigantic that far surpasses the tiny limits of the human mind. All of this action is the result of energetic hand acting at and from the source of all power, a benevolent hand of purpose.

While some action is outward, most is inward. The world cannot see the interior changes in believing, or perceiving, or thinking, or feeling, or deciding; no, the world can only see the exterior change in our behavior...our acting function. Yet, as the carpenter from Nazareth reminds us, "My kingdom is not of this world." My reading of this passage brings me to the fact that this Spirit of God acts most decisively in the bosom of my interior (page 207, Discover Your Spiritual Strengths: Find Health, Healing & Happiness).

Morning Prayer

Truth

Your truth is a lighthouse beacon keeping my direction straight and my actions sure.

I awaken this morning knowing that your truth is in me; that you offer me the grace that sets me free from my own distorted desires, which only feed my hurts.

Your truth elevates my behaviors in accordance with your guiding hand and sustains my actions in line with your divine honesty.

I am like a ship at sea that would be lost except for your truth that shines like a lighthouse beacon keeping my direction straight and my actions sure.

Your grace gathers up all the little disparate pieces of me and forms them together giving me integrity of mind and surety of action.

Truth sets me free from the clutter of distraction that encumbers my freedom of action in you.

I desire to be sure and true in you, Lord.

My heart's desire is to follow you all the days of my life and to be your hands and feet in this world.

Help me focus on the light of truth in me, the freedom-giving grace that heals my _____.

Amen

Afternoon Prayer

Deceit

The Shadow of Truth

Save me from playing with the truth.

Lord, save me from the slippery slope of fooling myself.

When I misplace your truth, I start down a road to self-deception.

I can slide into untruths without any conscious awareness of it until I crash head-on into the darkness of falsehood.

Save me from playing with the truth, manipulating it, and even from telling little "white" lies that can grow into full-pledged self-deception.

Help me to find the light of your truth that I may have blocked out with deceit.

This is the light that salves my hurting heart and heals my _____.

This is the light that illuminates my true intentions and gives resolve to my actions.

Save me from advancing untruths, from giving false witness, from bluffing myself, and from bending or circumventing the truth to achieve undeserved "reward."

Help me to take the risk of recognizing and telling your truth, Lord.

Amen

Evening Prayer

Skepticism

The Compulsion of Truth

Help me move away from doubting and into your light of truth.

I so desire truth Lord that at times I take on an overly-questioning mindset desperately trying to determine if any deception exists.

Skepticism has become my personal "default-position."

I so fear being lied to, being cheated, being gullible, and being seen as foolish that I find it hard to believe almost anything.

Lord, save me from seeing the motivations of others as manipulative, or even malevolent.

Help me move away from doubting and into your light of truth.

I find it so hard to believe others that I begin questioning myself, and forgive me, Lord I even question your motivations.

I'm dubious and have developed a critical attitude —all to avoid being deceived. I need your healing, Lord.

There is no power in this world that can cleanse this terrible curse from my soul; I need the power that only comes from you, the power of truth to heal my _____.

Light me up with your truth, Lord; brighten my world and heal me from myself.

Amen

Morning Prayer
Inspiration

Let my actions today be a testimony to your wonder-working power in my soul.

Lord, as the sun gently pushes away the darkness; infuse me with the light of your inspiration.

Illuminate my actions and help me become ever more aware of your presence in everything that I do, and everyone I meet today.

Let your inspirational light show me your real world and be my healing power.

Grant me the gift of inspiration to guide my hands and feet today, so that I can be about your business all day long.

Motivate me with your inaudible yet clear voice, and let me be the true inspired "me" as I move through this day.

Touch me with your mighty mechanisms of care, so that my actions reflect your healing power to me and to those around me.

Help me, Lord, to let go of any hurt that befuddles me and blocks your healing from my _____, so that I can be free to be with you and to act in your name.

Let my actions today be a testimony to your wonder-working power in my soul.

Amen

Afternoon Prayer

Deadened

The Shadow of Inspiration

Help me resist the terrible passivity that tugs at my heart.

Oh Lord, I ask for your love-energy of inspiration this afternoon, to overpower my proclivity toward lifelessness.

I need your light to overcome the lack of spirit that so often darkens my soul.

Help me resist the terrible passivity that tugs at my heart and dampens the vigor of your inspiration in me.

Let me accept your continuous grace of inspiration so I can act with resolve and purpose today and discover the meaning that you have hidden for me among the folds of my behavior.

Let me become more aware that I am dependent only on you and nothing or no one else.

Inspire my spirit to act as you would have me act today.

I need your inspiration so that I don't slip into an insipid morbidity, and consequently, put on-hold what is genuinely most important for healing my _____ now.

Amen

Evening Prayer

Excitability

The Compulsion of Inspiration

Grant me release from my need to live my life in constant motion.

Calm my body with your holy inspiration today, Lord, so that I may move beyond my desperate need for continuous stimulation.

Infuse my actions with your restful inspiring presence so I may move away from the ferocity of anxiousness and nervousness.

Your inspiration is a light from you that shines within me and heals my _____.

Inspiration propels me to new realms of peace and tranquility, to places of quiet and relaxation where my dismaying agitation is quenched by your soothing quiet words.

Give me the power to stop my perpetual movement with its frantic repetition, which infects my spirit with a terrible monotony as though I were on a treadmill going nowhere, instead of on a purposeful journey toward you.

Grant me release from my need to live my life in constant motion, a frenetic flutter of action going nowhere except to yet more senseless stimulation, all the while living in a wasteland of activity of going only in circles.

Inspire me so I can once again enjoy your quiet presence in me.

Amen

Morning Prayer
Kindness

You call me to be kind — to demonstrate gentle, affectionate, and loving behaviors.

Lord, today help me learn your ways of kindness.

Help me stay anchored in your kingdom but not forget your children's needs here on this earth as well.

Help me remain ever focused on the light of your grace; that grand and sublime kindness that soothes and heals my

_____.

Help me keep your healing light shining in me all day long.

Lord, you call me to be kind —to demonstrate gentle, affectionate, and loving behaviors.   Help me carry this out with a special understanding that my healing requires that I accept your words and carry-out the behaviors that flow from this surrender.

Your kindness calls me to help others, but let me not forget to be kind to myself as well.

Help me accept everything, and everyone, including myself, as gifts from you that deserve my holy attention.

Lord, help me to render care where it is needed, friendship where it's called for, and aide where it's most required.

Let me do all of this with respect and courteous goodwill.

Amen

Afternoon Prayer

Neglect

The Shadow of Kindness

Help me realize that my actions can and do make a difference.

I don't intentionally neglect anyone or anything, but I know that I can distance myself from you by my omissions.

Lord, help me to see the passive quality of neglect; it's what I don't do and when I don't act that bites at my soul.

I pray for your grace of kindness so I can give attention to those things, places, and people who need it.

Help me realize that my actions can and do make a difference, however small, and that your face is always present in everything.

Let me not ignore, isolate, or stonewall my efforts or those of others who wish to help.

Help me see how I may benignly neglect my own needs and requirements. Let me not disrespect or deny what is necessary for my continued growth toward you.

Open up my heart so I can be kind to myself during this time of healing.

My _____ needs the healing light of your kindness; help me do what I need to do to welcome your grace completely.

Amen

Evening Prayer

Co-Dependency

The Compulsion of Kindness

Save me from hovering over another in my vain efforts to make sure that all goes well.

Lord, help me realize when and how I'm becoming dependent on another person's dependencies.

Save me from over-stretching my efforts to help or support someone else I care for personally or serve professionally.

I can over-function at times and inadvertently and unnecessarily relieve others of responsibility for helping themselves.

Save me from hovering over another in my vain efforts to make sure that all goes well.

Help me let natural consequences bring more reasonable results even though there may be some pain in the short-run.

Help me not smother another but realize that kindness includes letting the other person take responsibility for his/her actions.

I cannot carry someone else's cross; I can only carry my own.

Lord, heal my _____ with your light of true kindness; save me from my proclivities of losing sight of the effects of my actions.

Amen

Morning Prayer
Courage

Let your courage saturate my personality.

Lord, the morning light reminds me of the immense internal fortitude that you have given me; you have planted your courage in me.

You call me to accept your healing of my _____ with resilience and hardiness, to hold out against its attacks…to be as tenacious as a bulldog.

Your grace gives me firmness of mind and the courage to venture forth even in the face of danger.

You make me dauntless, Lord.

My role is to open up my doorways of grace, so I can position my true self in such a way as to receive your power and might maximally.

My many hurts are echoes that one day I'm leaving this earth and journeying closer to you, part of my healing is to remember this unalterable fact.

Help me stand against the slings and barbs of my woundedness.

Let your courage saturate my personality so I may not fall into the temptation of my shadows and compulsions.

Amen

Afternoon Prayer

Timidity

The Shadow of Courage

Let your courage be the point of light that give me strength to continue.

Lord, I can become scared, faint of heart, and even lose the determination of courage that I know is your gift to me.

Give me the self-confidence to stop avoiding that which I must face; help me not 'run for cover' in the sometimes odd ways that I can.

Let me not shrink from carrying the cross I need to carry now.

Let your courage be the point of light that gives me strength to continue with inspiration.

Save me from letting fear send me into retreat, evading the hard truth of my woundedness and thereby prolonging the pain that it causes.

I pray for your courage to lift me from my tendency to shy away from what I know I must do, or dodge your sometimes-difficult offers to heal my _____.

Your courage can help me pull my head out of the sand and face fore square all that I need to face.

You are my strength, Lord. You are the light that eases my pain and brings healing.

Amen

Evening Prayer

Arrogance

The Compulsion of Courage

Give me the courage so I can drink the cup of my woundedness.

I can sometimes show a false courage by unknowingly creeping over into arrogance.

I can cop a condescending attitude and a superior tone.

Help me become more aware of the many ways that I do this and thus avoid the work of your true courage in me.

I can hide behind the bravado of arrogance to cover-up my inadequacies surrounding timidity.

I can puff myself up in an attempt to appear better than I am.

Help me from violations of caution, deliberation, and true consideration, where I am imprudent, careless, and sometimes stumble headlong into unnecessary or ill-conceived actions that I am later forced to defend or clean-up after.

Save me from the terrible *hubris* that can contort my soul.

Help me be more like you, Lord, showing the hard courage you did.

Give me that courage so I can drink the cup of my _____ and thereby move closer to your balm of healing.

Amen

Morning Prayer
Perseverance

Right now, in my hour of need, your perseverance sustains me.

Lord, I open my eyes this morning knowing that I have but one purpose: growing closer to you.

You hold me up with your perseverance, the grace to carry on, and your powerful tenacity in me that leads me to persistently plod on in my quest for you.

I thank you, Lord, for your gift to run the extra mile, to carry-on when hope is slim, to stay the course even when I see only darkly through the lens of life.

Right now, in my hour of need, I know your perseverance is there to sustain me.

Your perseverance surprises me because I know that this is not my power, but your power in me that enables me to find healing while carrying this heavy cross.

Perseverance is the point of light that heals my _____.

Perseverance animates my actions and activates my true spiritual grit to keep going and to keep fully on the task of healing with stamina and backbone.

I am filled with awe at the power you have invested in me.

Amen

Afternoon Prayer

Giving Up

The Shadow of Perseverance

Lord, help me stay engaged and not desist.

Oh, how I sometimes want to surrender, not to you Lord, but to my failings.

I want to withdraw from "action," throw in the towel, and simply walk away.

But then I remember your gift of perseverance; I can then get up, gain my footing, and begin my journey back to you again.

Help me stay engaged and not desist, help me stay in the "game" and not prematurely terminate my efforts before my time.

I can overcome my exhaustion with your perseverance; I can persist and not submit to my vulnerabilities of giving up too soon.

Lord, help me know the difference between the growth of surrendering (falling in) to you, and stagnation of surrendering to my pain.

Your light of perseverance illuminates my actions so that they point only to you.

Let me not take the counsel of the world and retreat without just cause. Grant me the perseverance to come to you for healing my _____.

Amen

Evening Prayer

Imperiousness

The Compulsion of Perseverance

Lord, help me see that I don't need to be a martyr.

Lord, help to recognize the times when I am unnecessarily endangering myself and/or others.

I don't want to be in jeopardy, but I fear that, even without my conscious awareness, I can take actions (or inactions) that place what I love in danger.

Save me from these tendencies of action, help me persevere in your love, and remain open to your grace that fortifies me in body, mind, and spirit.

Help me see that I don't have to "go down with the ship." I don't need to be a martyr.

Your grace is the only power than can save me from this illogical perversion of your strength of perseverance.

Imperiousness is not strong; it is a compulsive act to get me beyond my fear of giving-up.

I know I'm not a quitter, but I needn't prove it to myself or anyone else, and certainly not to you, Lord, by unnecessarily "playing with fire." Let perseverance be my light to come to you, to heal my _____.

Amen

Postlude

You must be persistent in your prayer for it to become maximally effective in your walk with _____. When you regularly and continuously pray, you increase your receptivity to God's healing power.

"We are to pray in everyday life, and we are to make everyday life our prayer." (Rahner, page 45).

- Prayer does not insure that you will be insulated from the trials and tribulations of your _____.

- Yet, prayer does offer you the spiritual potentials of strength, perseverance, and spiritual stamina so you may remain steadfast in faith and calm of demeanor regardless of the personal travails of your _____ walk.

- Prayer is your stimulus to grow in the face of human conflict; prayer is not a means of avoiding the conflict.

- Prayer offers no escape hatch from your worldly duties and responsibilities of _____, whether that is as a _____ patient or as a _____ caregiver.

- Prayer does offer a magnificent means for vigorously entering into the fray of your _____ predicament and yet, at the same time, prayer offers you a new calmness and a peaceful detachment from the outcome of the fray.

Go in peace to serve the Lord and find immense healing.

Appendix

Assumptions of the Spiritual Strengths Healing Plan

- Healing is best understood to proceed along all three levels of human experience: 1) body, 2) mind, and 3) spirit. **Maximal healing is achieved wholistically**, i.e., each of these three levels of human experience must be addressed as a part of a larger unit ...as part of a whole, which is more than the three parts taken individually.

- The "mind" portion of the wholistic perspective of healing is seen in the Spiritual Strengths Healing Plan as the **six operational functions of the personality**: 1) believing, 2) perceiving, 3) thinking, 4) feeling, 5) deciding, and 6) acting.

- The "Spirit" portion of the wholistic perspective is seen in the Spiritual Strengths Healing Plan as the special or **premier spiritual strength** (virtue) you have received in each of the six functions of your personality. You have been given one premier gift in each of the six functions for a total of six spiritual strengths ...your special healing type ...your spiritual fingerprint.

- **Love** is the fundamental healing power; all energy flows from this central font of the power of Love. Love comes from God; it cannot be manufactured or synthesized by humans.

- **Healing** is clearly distinguished from the medical concept of **curing**. Curing means restoring physical brokenness or malfunctioning **(sickness)** to a state of functionality. Healing, on the other hand, is seen as closing the gap in mind and/or spirit that was opened by your reactions to your sickness. This gap, usually expressed through personality pain, is what is called **illness**.

- The more completely you can **open-up** to the healing power of God within you, the more you will benefit from these gifts of grace.

- You have been endowed with spiritual strengths that are **particular, singular, specific, and unique** to you.

- These personal spiritual strengths serve as your **primary means of achieving healing** and personal spiritual growth.

- As you become increasingly **aware of your spiritual strengths**, you will quite naturally begin the process of folding the power of your spiritual strengths into your everyday life.

- Each of your spiritual strengths has a corresponding **shadow**, a condition where the spiritual strength is absent. This shadow presents a special vulnerability or possible point of internal tension in you.

- Likewise, each of your spiritual strengths has a corresponding **compulsion**, a condition where your ego has distended the strength to a point of distortion. This compulsion becomes a proclivity in you to move away from your spiritual strength and consequently away from your Real Self.

- When shadows are brought to light, and compulsions are revealed as personality "terrorists", healing work quite naturally commences on the task of using your shadows and/or compulsions **in service of your healing** and enhanced spiritual growth.

- The Spiritual Strengths Healing Plan is **not "faith healing"** where you rely on your internal mechanisms as the sole means for physical cure. **The Spiritual Strengths Healing Plan never promises cure**; its purpose is healing. The Method can however be seen as a supplement and support for traditional medical practices. The philosophy of the Spiritual Strengths Healing Plan is that you should seek the best and most appropriate medical and psychological care you can in accord with your own personal wishes.

21020423R00079

Made in the USA
San Bernardino, CA
03 May 2015